JESUS' BIBLE

JESUS' BIBLE

A CONCISE HISTORY OF THE HEBREW SCRIPTURES

Christopher Dost

JESUS' BIBLE
A CONCISE HISTORY OF THE HEBREW SCRIPTURES

© 2018 by Christopher Dost

ISBN-13: 9781793849236

First printing, November 2018.
Second printing, with minor revisions, January 2019.

Published by Kindle Direct Publishing.

All translations of biblical texts are the author's own. Where indicated, quotations of the Aramaic Targums are printed with the permission of OakTree Software. Quotations of the Babylonian Talmud are excerpted from Jacob Neusner, ed., *The Babylonian Talmud: A Translation and Commentary on CD* (Peabody, MA: Hendrickson, 2010) with the permission of Hendrickson Publishers. Quotations of the Jerusalem Talmud are excerpted from Jacob Neusner, ed., *The Jerusalem Talmud: A Translation and Commentary on CD* (Peabody, MA: Hendrickson, 2010) with the permission of Hendrickson Publishers.

Cover design by Rachel Lee.

TABLE OF CONTENTS

Preface   i
Abbreviations   v

Introduction   Why This Book?   1
Chapter 1   The Masoretic Text   15
Chapter 2   Biblical Hebrew   33
Chapter 3   Israel & Judah's Past: History & Historiography   39
Chapter 4   The Hebrew Bible as Literature   51
Chapter 5   Literacy & Text Production   63
Chapter 6   Who Wrote the Bible?   73
Chapter 7   The Bible in Translation, Part 1: The Targums   93
Chapter 8   The Bible in Translation, Part 2: The Septuagint   105
Conclusion   117

Bibliography   119

PREFACE

Many Christians are keenly interested in learning about the origins of the Old Testament (or the Hebrew Bible, as biblical scholars prefer to call it), in part because certain statements within the Christian Bible's two Testaments seem to indicate that the writing of Scripture was a mystical process.[1] While there are many good scholarly works that shed light on this process, there are, to my knowledge, no up-to-date, well-researched works that present the story of the Hebrew Bible's composition, growth, and finalization in a way that the non-expert can appreciate. I hope that this book helps to fill this void.

From the outset, I must be clear that my aim in writing this book is not theological. There is an abundance of works that discuss the various perspectives on the question of the divine inspiration of the Hebrew Scriptures. I leave this dialogue to the theologians. I write, instead, as an historian, exploring the *human* contribution to the Hebrew Scriptures, because such knowledge can help one to better understand why the Hebrew Bible was written in the first place.

My own curiosity in this subject was piqued about twenty years ago when a minister pointed out to me that in certain instances, the New International Version (NIV), like many other modern English translations, lacks words and phrases that are found in the King James Version (KJV), my preferred translation at the time. The NIV's shorter readings, he explained, result from the translators' decision to follow ancient manuscripts that differed in wording from those on which the KJV was ultimately based. As a result, I became curious to learn about the process of the transmission of the Bible. Who were the original authors? How did biblical books make it from the original authors to us, the modern readers?

---

[1]   E.g., 2 Timothy 3:16; 2 Peter 1:20-21.

My curiosity was aroused all the more when I realized that many of the New Testament's quotations of the Hebrew Bible did not match the corresponding passages in my Bible's Old Testament. As I began to study the Old and New Testaments in their original languages (Hebrew, Aramaic, and Greek), these two questions became somewhat of a preoccupation for me and ultimately drove me to write this book. It is my hope that everyone who reads this book, regardless of his or her faith commitments or lack thereof, will find within these pages an engaging and informative introduction to the questions of how the Old Testament was produced and what it looked like in Jesus' day.

The publication of this work would not have been possible without the assistance of many individuals. First and foremost, I wish to thank Michelle Dost, who aided me substantively in virtually every aspect of this work, including artistic design, conceptual development, and proofreading. Rimon Armaly, Chase Connolly, Julianne Cox, Karen Dost, Mark Dost, Heidi Fagan, Jeffrey Hoops, Jason Lee, David Marcus, Sara Pereyra, Nestor Soto, and Jim Welty provided many suggestions that led to the significant improvement of this book. I offer special thanks to Viktor Golinets and Bella Hass Weinberg, whose contributions to this monograph are numerous. Any errors and shortcomings that remain are, of course, my own responsibility.

This work is dedicated to the memory of my grandmother, Anna Louise Dost.

LIST OF ABBREVIATIONS

ABH	Archaic Biblical Hebrew
Aram.	Aramaic
ABD	*Anchor Bible Dictionary*
b.	The Babylonian Talmud
BCE	Before the Common Era
BHS	*Biblia Hebraica Stuttgartensia*
BHQ	*Biblia Hebraica Quinta*
ca.	Circa
CE	Common Era
cf.	Compare
CHE	*The Chronicle of Higher Education*
COS	*The Context of Scripture*
DSS	Dead Sea Scrolls
Grk.	Greek
Heb.	Hebrew
JANT	*The Jewish Annotated New Testament*
KAI	*Kanaanäische und Aramäische Inschriften*
KJV	King James Version
Lat.	Latin
LBH	Late Biblical Hebrew
LXX	Septuagint
m.	Mishna
M	Masoretic Text Family
NIV	New International Version
NT	New Testament
OT	Old Testament
R.	Rabbi/Rav
SBH	Standard Biblical Hebrew
TBH	Transitional Biblical Hebrew
TCHB[3]	*Textual Criticism of the Hebrew Bible*, 3d ed.
y.	Jerusalem Talmud

WHY THIS BOOK?

Think not that I am come to destroy the law,[1] or the prophets: I am not come to destroy, but to fulfil. For verily I say unto you, till heaven and earth pass, one jot or one tittle shall in no wise pass from the law, till all be fulfilled.

—Matthew 5:17-18 (KJV)

Jots and Tittles

The jot and the tittle are the smallest features of Hebrew script. The Greek word translated as "jot" (*iota*) refers to the letter *yod* ('), the tiniest letter of the Hebrew alphabet; and the Greek word in Matthew 5:18 translated as "tittle" (*keraia*) refers to a small stroke or flourish added to certain Hebrew letters.[2] So according to Jesus, there is great significance in even the tiniest elements of the script of the Hebrew Bible.

---

[1] While "law" is generally a fine translation for the Greek word used here in Matthew's Gospel, Jesus surely has in mind the Hebrew concept of "Torah," which is better thought of as God's "Instruction" rather than his "Law."

[2] Lightfoot, *A Commentary on the New Testament from the Talmud and Hebraica*, 2:100-102; Strack & Billerbeck, *Kommentar zum neuen Testament aus Talmud und Midrash*, 1:244; *JANT*, 10. It is likely that the Greek term corresponds to the Aramaic word *tagin*, which are flourishes that ornament seven different Hebrew letters (Yeivin, *Introduction to the Tiberian Masorah*, 38). The crown-like flourishes in Torah scrolls are a second-millennium CE attempt at reconstructing the *tagin* mentioned in rabbinic sources that date to the first century CE (Ardeni, *The Book of Hebrew Script: History, Paleography, Script Styles, Calligraphy, and Design*, 210).

The Babylonian Talmud presents a similar claim:

Be attentive to your work, for your craft does the
work of Heaven. Should you leave out a single letter
or add a single letter [to a document], you will turn
out to destroy an entire world.[3]

These two texts—one from the Christian[4] Scriptures and one
from Jewish sacred literature—both greatly revere the Hebrew
Bible and hold that even its smallest details are of the greatest
significance.[5] For these two religious traditions, the least
regarded of God's commandments are as important as those that
are most highly regarded.[6] But in addition, they both seem to
expect that manuscripts containing the word of God should be
copied and passed on to subsequent generations[7] with the
greatest of care.

Most words in the English language have only one
correct spelling, but there are some that have more than one. The
Massachusetts town that is home to the New England Patriots
can be spelled with the full, older spelling "Foxborough" or with

---

[3]   B. Sota 20a (Neusner). The Babylonian Talmud is a collection of
rabbinic discourse from the first six centuries CE, which was recorded in
writing sometime around the seventh century CE. In this book, citations of the
Babylonian Talmud begin with the abbreviation "b."

[4]   We shall discuss the Jewishness of the New Testament later in this
work. Until then, I refer to all of the writings of the New Testament as
"Christian" for the sake of convenience.

[5]   The rabbis were even interested in whether a compound word should
be written as one word or two, as is the case with the form יְדִידְיָה ("Jedediah")
in 2 Samuel 12:25. The Masoretes do not agree on this matter, and that is
probably influenced by the following rabbinic discussion: "Said R. Hisda said
R. Yohanan, 'The words, hallelujah, kesjah (Exodus 17:16) and yedidyah
(2 Samuel 12:25) are single words.'...*The question was asked: as to yedidyah
from the perspective of Rab, what is the situation? Come and take note, for*
said Rab, 'Yedidyah is divided into two, so the Yedid part is secular, the Yah
part is sacred'" (b. Pesah. 117a, Neusner).

[6]   Kugel, *The Bible as It Was*, 519-20.

[7]   I use the term "transmit" to refer to the process of copying, editing,
and modifying the documents that comprise the Hebrew Bible.

an abridged, more modern spelling "Foxboro." In the Hebrew Bible, there are countless words that have more than one spelling. The Hebrew word for "prophets," for instance, is spelled three different ways in the Hebrew Bible: נביאים (Numbers 11:29); נבאים (1 Samuel 10:10); נביאם (1 Samuel 19:24). Even readers who have not studied Hebrew will observe that the second and third spellings each lack one instance of the Hebrew letter *yod* (י). Similarly, the word for "generations" also has more than one spelling. The word is spelled תולדות in Genesis 2:4, תולדת in Genesis 5:1, תלדות in Genesis 36:1, and תלדת in Genesis 25:12. All four spellings are pronounced the same way, however: *toledot*. The only difference between these four spellings is the presence or absence of the vowel letter "o" (ו).[8] The letter is optional because Hebrew script often leaves out vowel letters, expecting the reader to supply them, as is the case in modern Hebrew[9] and Arabic.

Coming from a theological perspective, the rabbis take a keen interest in such variations of spelling because they believe that God communicates even through the presence or absence of a seemingly optional letter, even when, from a human perspective, the spelling (or "orthography" as scholars sometimes refer to it) is mistaken.[10] For example, they note that only two instances of the word "generations" are spelled with two instances of the letter *vav* (ו). Because the letter ו also serves as the Hebrew number six, it is concluded that the "six" that is absent from all other forms of the word corresponds to six things that were lost when Adam sinned (Genesis 3:6).[11] To the rabbis,

---

[8]   Similarly, the Talmud (*b. Sanhedrin* 4b) discusses variant spellings of the word *totafot*, and, interestingly, the spelling that the Talmud presents for certain forms does not match that of the Masoretic text (e.g., Exodus 13:16). I thank Bella Hass Weinberg for this insight.

[9]   Modern Hebrew is characterized by full or longer spelling to facilitate pronunciation and comprehension.

[10]   Satlow, *Creating Judaism: History, Tradition, Practice*, 129.

[11]   Bereshit Rabba 12.6.

then, the spelling of each Hebrew word in the Bible is divinely inspired.

As I have noted above, many Christians also hold the Hebrew Bible in similar regard, which often gives rise to assumptions about the Bible itself. One Hebrew Bible scholar argues that if biblical manuscripts have not been preserved accurately, then numerous Christian beliefs may rightly be called into question.[12] And indeed, it is reasonable for the Christian to ask how he or she can confidently believe teachings derived from Scripture if the biblical texts on which they are based have not been preserved correctly. For this reason, conservative Christians have taken great interest in defending the accuracy of the Scriptures. The reasoning on which many of them base their bibliology (i.e., theology of the Bible itself) rests on assumptions that cannot be substantiated, however. A common argument goes something like this:

> Scripture must be letter-perfect (accurate down to the very letter) if the major doctrines of conservative Christianity are true. Since personal religious experience confirms that biblical teachings are true, then it stands to reason that the texts on which they are based are letter-perfect. And if they are letter-perfect, they must accurately preserve the word of God and are therefore reliable in all matters.

This is a generalization, of course, but a fair one.

The extent to which the Hebrew Bible is reliable, trustworthy, and accurate is hotly debated within conservative Christianity, and it is one that has led to sharp dissension. This is well documented in Matthew Barrett's 2016 work *God's Word Alone: The Authority of Scripture*, which is published by

---

[12] Kaiser, *The Old Testament Documents: Are They Reliable and Relevant?* 41. Unfortunately, he, like many other evangelical writers (as we shall see below), paints a picture of Old Testament texts that is based upon very dated sources and that is therefore out of touch with recent developments in scholarship.

a leading evangelical press. The work is immensely valuable for its historical sketch of the debate over the accuracy and authority of Scripture, but it does not fairly present alternative perspectives and may therefore mislead the reader.[13]

The battlefield of this debate is not only the printed page but also the academy. In 2018, the year following the five hundredth anniversary of the Protestant Reformation, Moody Bible Institute decided to adopt the 1978 Chicago Statement on Biblical Inerrancy,[14] requiring all faculty to affirm it in its entirety. The Statement, however, is only one voice from the evangelical camp and is no more than an affirmation of one theological *tradition*'s understanding of the Bible.[15] But more than that, it is a one-size-fits-all approach to every text within the anthology of Scripture, which, as we will see later, resists such reductionism. For those who work closely with Hebrew Bible manuscripts, perhaps the most troubling aspect of the Statement is Article 10, which rightly acknowledges that the Hebrew and Aramaic manuscripts available today are not the

---

[13]   Barrett's work is ultimately a flawed defense of a Reformed perspective on Scripture. For instance, he criticizes his fellow evangelicals who attempt to objectively read biblical texts in the light of historical, social, and linguistic context because their approach to biblical interpretation was not revealed by God himself (224). Yet he himself has to resort to reason—not divine revelation—in order to defend the Reformed views of the infallibility and inerrancy of Scripture because the Bible does not make such claims about itself, nor can it be expected to, seeing as how all of the documents that comprise the Bible were written at a time when there was not yet a Bible, a fact which he regularly seems to forget! Furthermore, Barrett's discussion of biblical manuscripts reveals that he does not understand the problems that data culled from Hebrew Bible manuscripts pose for his views of the Bible (266-67), and this undermines his overall credibility. If theologians such as Barrett were to first study biblical manuscripts before earnestly contending for their theological presuppositions, their theology of the Bible would be greatly transformed. For a brief overview and assessment of *God's Word Alone*, see Miller, "Review of Matthew Barrett, *God's Word Alone*," 257-59.

[14]   Published in Geisler, ed., *Inerrancy*, 1980.

[15]   See, for instance, point 4 of the Short Statement (ibid., 494).

original but incorrectly suggests that they are close to the original manuscripts, or, as scholars sometimes call them, the "autographs."[16] The concept of "the original" to which the signatories of the Statement hold is not a recoverable text, at least as far as the Hebrew Bible is concerned. And even if we could recover it, it would scarcely resemble what the signatories have in mind, as we shall see in chapters 5 and 6. Virtually all scholars who make a career out of studying Hebrew Bible manuscripts have completely given up on the idea of the autograph.

While the Hebrew Bible has been transmitted in a fairly reliable fashion, scholarship has convincingly demonstrated that errors and emendations of various types have been part of the transmission process from the start. Whatever one's theological presuppositions, it is imperative that any responsible student of Scripture and theology be aware of such developments in the field.

Scholarship has long taken for granted that the Hebrew Bible was still in a somewhat fluid state even in the final years of the Second Temple period—the period that stretches from the dedication of Jerusalem's second temple around 515 BCE through the period to which Christians often refer as the "Intertestamental" period or "the 400 silent years,"[17] to the temple's destruction in 70 CE. Even at this relatively late period, it had not yet reached the final form now available to us in printed editions. David Marcus and James A. Sanders note that during this time no "letter perfect" biblical texts existed, and the Dead Sea Scrolls bear this out.[18] Even if one grants Waltke's estimation that substantial problems are limited to less than ten

---

[16]   Ibid., 496.
[17]   In chapter 6, we will see that these years were far from silent.
[18]   Marcus & Sanders, "What's Critical about a Critical Edition of the Bible?" 63. Many conservative Christians may find it striking that the religious faithful at Qumran held a very high view of Scripture but at the same time accepted that manuscripts of the same Hebrew text could be wildly divergent from one another.

percent of the Hebrew Bible, it is still not a perfect text.[19] The Hebrew Bible of the Second Temple period was textually corrupt.

If conservative Christian scholarship is well aware that each of the individual manuscripts of the Hebrew Bible are textually corrupt, and they assume that it is only the non-extant (i.e., no longer in existence) *autographs*—the original handwritten copies of each individual book—that are inerrant, what is the problem? Brogan notes that many evangelicals who should know better nevertheless equate the autographic ideal with the corrupt form of the biblical texts used today. Such a notion could not be more at variance with the present state of Old Testament scholarship.[20] The plurality of textual traditions among the Qumran manuscripts coupled with new findings from research of scribal culture have lead many in the field to conclude that the evangelical conception of Old Testament autographs is nothing more than fantasy.

Why This Book?

Just from the sources in the bibliography, one can see that there is no shortage of books that address the origins and development of the Hebrew Bible/Old Testament. So why this book? Most of the students that I teach are evangelical Christians who are preparing or further equipping themselves for one type of ministry or another. Many of them have in the course of their higher education studied the Bible in a non-confessional (i.e., non-religious) way, often to fulfill one of their undergraduate religion or literature requirements. At most colleges and universities, such courses teach mainstream scholarly approaches to the Scriptures, such as those discussed in the following chapters, and many of my seminary-level students

---

19   Waltke, "Old Testament Textual Criticism," 157.
20   Brogan, "Can I Have Your Autograph? Uses and Abuses of Textual Criticism in Formulating an Evangelical Doctrine of Scripture," 100-101; Wilson, "Canon and Theology: What is at Stake?" 242.

have learned to read the Bible according to these approaches before they ever stepped foot in my classroom. It is my job to continue to educate them in scholarly methods and perspectives while also helping them to think critically about what it all means for their faith commitments. Much of what is written in this book has arisen from discussions that have taken place with students inside and outside of my classroom.

As for my students who have not taken such courses, most of them have been introduced to the perspectives of mainstream biblical scholarship through the media, whether by watching a History Channel documentary that questions the historical accuracy of the Old Testament's narrative, a New York Times op-ed that raises doubts as to whether the book of Leviticus initially proscribed male homosexuality or not,[21] or perhaps an interview with New Testament scholar Bart Ehrman on The Daily Show that addresses the role scribes played in adding material to biblical texts. So, all of my students, in one way or another, have encountered mainstream biblical scholarship prior to commencing their seminary education.

Some of these aforementioned media productions are responsible treatments of this difficult subject matter and do a fantastic job of informing the general public of the problems that biblical scholars face in reconstructing the history of the Bible. Others, however, are more sensationalist in nature and thus much less useful. Addressing the extensive sensationalist media attention given to the Dead Sea Scrolls, for instance, Schiffman laments that such productions "have tended to invert reality…" and that the media ultimately "(mis)shape public perception."[22] The media can do as much bad as good.

It is not only the sensationalist media productions that are to blame for misperceptions of the Hebrew Bible's origins and development, however. There are a number of popular works on this subject written by authors who have not been

[21] See Dershowitz, "The Secret History of Leviticus."
[22] Schiffman, *Qumran and Jerusalem: Studies in the Dead Sea Scrolls and the History of Judaism*, 411, 412.

trained in biblical studies at an advanced level, whose respective works exhibit limited awareness of biblical scholarship and do more to reinforce common misunderstandings about the Bible than to introduce the reader to what is actually known. One of the better works that fit this category is Philip Yancey's, *The Bible Jesus Read*. Yancey's aim is to encourage Christians to read the Hebrew Bible and to grow in appreciation for the way in which its millennia-old content can still impact readers today. In my estimation, Yancey does well to invite the reader into a dialogue with the Hebrew Scriptures, but there are three aspects of the book that are of concern. First, to call the Hebrew Bible "the Bible Jesus read" is not entirely accurate, as I have already indicated. There was no Bible in Jesus' day. The Torah and the Prophets—the first two sections of what would become the Hebrew Bible—were essentially canonized (i.e., accepted as authoritative), but they were still textually fluid. The third section, however, the Writings, was not fixed. Thus, there was no "Bible." Second, understanding Jesus' Bible is just as much an investigation into *how* Jesus read as it is of *what* he read, a subject that Yancey barely touches. The third aspect of this work that raises alarm concerns method. Before giving an interpretation of a text, it is important that the interpreter follow a reliable method or a procedure that allows him or her to confidently interpret the biblical text under consideration. Yancey notes in the preface that he is not interested in or qualified to evaluate scholarly investigations of the dating and authorship of biblical books, preferring instead to read the Bible from a lay perspective.[23] I admire Yancey for his honesty, and I do believe that he generally reads the *translated* Hebrew Bible in a responsible fashion. Yet one of my principal reasons for writing this work is that the matters that Yancey has decided to avoid are essential for producing a reliable interpretation of any biblical text and are necessary for reconstructing the history of the Hebrew Scriptures.

---

[23]   Yancey, *The Bible Jesus Read*, 9.

This unfortunate state of affairs is further exacerbated by the fact that those who are competent to write such works generally do not do so because their institution does not reward faculty for engaging with the broader public[24] and/or because they are afraid of the backlash that they could face from their institution's administration and constituency, finding it safer to keep quiet than to share knowledge with those outside of the field. Therefore, many non-specialists who are interested in learning about the Bible's origins do not know where to turn for a fair, non-sensationalist treatment of the material. In fact, many of my religiously conservative students have expressed to me their frustration over the Church's failure to discuss these "other perspectives" and to engage with those who hold them. There was a time when conservative Christianity could bury its proverbial head in the sand, but that time is long past. While the Hebrew Bible/Old Testament may be a very ancient anthology, written at a time and in a place very distant from the reader's own, understanding its origins and its message is immensely important even in the twenty-first century for political and cultural reasons. As I have indicated above, this dialogue does not only take place within academic institutions. A fairly recent History Channel documentary raises the question of whether the Old Testament can be taken as literal truth and explains that how one answers the question has bearings on one's views on human origins, sexuality, and abortion.[25]

Ultimately, this book's objective is to help the non-specialist better understand what the Hebrew Scriptures looked like in their various iterations before they became *the* Hebrew Bible in the Middle Ages. It is intended to be a concise presentation of the breadth of scholarship that deals with the history of the transmission of the Hebrew Bible, with the aim of helping the non-specialist become acquainted with many

---

[24] See Neil deGrasse Tyson's candid assessment of the situation in *CHE* vol. LXV, num. 3, A6, 9/21/2018.
[25] Ragobert, *The Bible Unearthed: The Making of a Religion,* episode 4.

important scholarly works and their contributions. The bibliography covers a wide range of scholarly opinion, from the ultra-liberal to the ultra-conservative.[26] It is my hope that presenting a cross-section of the field of scholarship will also equip the reader to more profitably engage with scholarship and those who hold views different from his or her own.[27]

---

[26] Whenever possible, I prefer to avoid the terms "liberal" and "conservative," as they have a fairly broad array of connotations, some of which are denigrative. When discussing matters of history, scholarship uses the terms "minimalist" and "maximalist" for those who, respectively, have significantly less or significantly more confidence in the historical reliability of biblical texts.

[27] I have been disheartened to see that much of the literature produced for broader evangelical audiences tends to be simply apologetic in nature—that is to say, concerned with defending the faith—and less concerned with fostering meaningful dialogue with those who hold other positions. It is not uncommon in these works for writers to misrepresent, caricature, and sometimes disparage mainstream scholarship and those who hold unorthodox views. Many of my readers are familiar with one edition or another of Josh McDowell and Sean McDowell's *Evidence that Demands a Verdict*, which is a work of Christian apologetics in which the authors argue for the credibility of Christianity in a format accessible to a broad readership. Their goal is to equip the reader to deal with a gamut of objections to the Christian faith. They seek to safeguard the reader from the many shortcomings of mainstream biblical scholarship and its deleterious effects on the faith of Christians, and to prepare Christians theologically and apologetically (xiv). I admire the authors for their commitment to their faith and to the dissemination of knowledge to a broader audience, something that mainstream scholarship does not do well. And the book is quite useful in that it familiarizes the non-expert with many important "facts" about the Bible. However, it is clear from the very first page of the preface that the authors are not above caricaturing and misrepresenting biblical scholarship, and this brings their credibility into question (e.g., xiii). To compound matters, it is immediately obvious that certain matters are not well-researched. This is evident from their assumptions about the nature of Moses' education in Egyptian universities (4), for example. As we shall see later in our discussion of the scribal culture of ancient Egypt, there were no universities in ancient Egypt. Such careless comments do not equip the reader; quite the contrary! The point, though, is that even the most well-meaning authors can paint quite distorted pictures of the Hebrew Bible and of scholarship, and this is ultimately a disservice to the Church.

Outline of the Book

The principal concern of this book is to survey the history of the Hebrew Scriptures from the earliest phases of composition in the late second millennium BCE through the tenth century CE, when the final form of the Hebrew Bible, the one that is most commonly used today, was completed. Over the course of this book's eight chapters we will consider why there was more than one accepted version of the Hebrew Scriptures in Jesus' day and how the versions differ from the received Hebrew text found in most modern printed editions.

In chapter one, "The Masoretic Text," I introduce the reader to the Tiberian Masoretic Hebrew Bible, the Bible that most have in mind when they refer to "the original Hebrew." This is for most traditions the final form and the *textus receptus* (Lat., "received text") of the Hebrew Bible.

Chapters two through five explore four areas of research that shed light on the Hebrew Bible's origins and growth. Chapter two briefly sketches the different phases of biblical Hebrew and how analysis of the Hebrew of a given text can provide clues as to when and where the text was written. Chapter three considers the historical reliability of the Hebrew Scriptures and their use for reconstructing ancient Israel's past. I compare what the Hebrew Bible says about Israel and Judah's past with what scholars consider to be true as a result of textual and archaeological investigation. This overview of Israelite and Judean history will be of use in more reliably locating the authors, editors, and copyists of Scripture within the broader history of the biblical people. In chapter four I consider the implications that reading the Hebrew Bible as ancient Near Eastern literature has for establishing the date and provenance (i.e., place of origin) of biblical texts. Chapter five explores scribal culture in the ancient Near East and the light it can shed on ancient Israelite scribal practices and text production.

In chapter six I turn to the question of who wrote the Hebrew Bible, comparing traditional assumptions about the authors of the Hebrew Scriptures with the results of scholarly inquiry. Chapters seven and eight discuss the two most important ancient translations of the Hebrew Bible: the Aramaic Targums and the Septuagint. These two chapters explore the reasons for translating the Hebrew Scriptures, the nature of those translations, and what they reveal about the state of biblical texts and their interpretation in Jesus' day. The book then closes with a brief conclusion.

Presentation

Before moving on to the first chapter, I would like to say a few words about this book's style of presentation. First, because the book is intended for a broader audience, I avoid using technical vocabulary as much as possible. When it is necessary to use shoptalk, I explain technical terms in parentheses or in footnotes. I also refrain from abbreviating the names of biblical books, since some readers may be less familiar than others with the contents of the Bible. Finally, in keeping with my stated aim, I include in this work numerous references to the sources that I have used in preparing this work. Typically, books written for a broader audience tend to cite sources only sparsely. I have decided to make constant reference to scholarly sources so that the reader may know where to continue the investigation of a topic about which (s)he desires to learn more.

1
THE MASORETIC TEXT

For the average Bible reader, the Hebrew Scriptures are little more than an abstraction. The non-specialist, in my experience, generally assumes that the Old Testament translation that he or she reads is a faithful representation of "the original Hebrew." It would seem that this idea is based upon the common assumption that figures such as David, Solomon, Joshua, Samuel, Job, and Isaiah wrote the books of the Bible that bear their names, and that these documents were copied and passed on (or transmitted) accurately until finally they were rendered faithfully into English. As we shall see in the course of our investigation, such was not the case. Each book of the Hebrew Bible has a complex literary history (some more complex than others), and the original form of very few, if any, of them resembled the version preserved in the Masoretic text, the Hebrew Bible on which modern English translations are principally based. Furthermore, none of the manuscripts available to us today ("extant," as we like to say in the field) were copied completely accurately, a subject that we shall take up in some detail later in the book. However, before we begin our chronological exploration of how the Hebrew Bible developed, let us have a look at the final form of the Hebrew Scriptures—the Tiberian Masoretic Hebrew Bible of the Ben Asher School—so that we can appreciate where this book is ultimately headed.

The Tiberian Masoretic Hebrew Bible
Let's begin by carefully defining what is meant by "The Tiberian Masoretic Hebrew Bible." First of all, it is a Bible. It consists of twenty-four books canonized within the Jewish tradition, which are separated into three divisions: the Torah, the Prophets, and the Writings. The Torah (lit., "instruction"), which is often

referred to as the "Law" (from the Greek translation "*nomos*") or the "Pentateuch," consists of the first five books of the Hebrew Scriptures: Genesis, Exodus, Leviticus, Numbers, and Deuteronomy.

The second division, the Prophets (Heb. *nevi'im*), consists of eight books, which are organized into two subdivisions. The first is the Former Prophets, which consists of Joshua, Judges, Samuel, and Kings. Christian readers may find this surprising for a few reasons. First, in the Christian tradition, Samuel and Kings are not two texts but four: 1 Samuel, 2 Samuel, 1 Kings, and 2 Kings. Second, in the Christian tradition, the book of Ruth is included between Judges and Samuel. But even more surprising to many Christians is that these works are classified as prophetic works, not historical.

The second subdivision is the Latter Prophets, which also consists of four books: Isaiah, Jeremiah, Ezekiel, and the Book of the Twelve. This is slightly different from the Protestant Christian canon. First, Lamentations is not included among the Prophets in the Jewish tradition. Second, the Book of the Twelve, which is commonly known by Christians as the "Minor Prophets," are thirteen individual books in the Protestant Canon: Daniel, Hosea, Joel, Amos, Obadiah, Jonah, Micah, Nahum, Habakkuk, Zephaniah, Haggai, Zechariah, and Malachi. In the Jewish tradition, the Minor Prophets are only twelve, as Daniel, like Ruth and Lamentations, is relegated to the third division of the Bible.

Finally, the third division is known as the "Writings" (Heb. *ketuvim*), which is a catch-all for anything not included in the Torah and the Prophets. The order of these books differs within the manuscripts and printed editions, but the canonical list is the same. I present them here according to their order in the famed Leningrad Codex, which is the text upon which most scholarly editions of the Hebrew Bible are based: Chronicles (as one book, not two), Psalms, Job, Proverbs, Ruth, Song of Songs, Ecclesiastes, Lamentations, Esther, Daniel, Ezra-Nehemiah (as one book, not two).

The tripartite (i.e., three-part) Hebrew Bible is often known by the acronym "Tanak" (or "Tanakh"). The "T" stands for Torah, the "N" for Nevi'im, and the "K" for Ketuvim. These are the contents of the Tiberian Masoretic Hebrew Bible. As I explain in some detail in chapter 5, the list (or "canon") of twenty-four books that constitute the Hebrew Bible was not settled once and for all until around the early seventh century CE. To be sure, many of these texts were considered authoritative before Jesus' day, but the canonicity of many of the Writings and a number of works that eventually did not make the cut was debated for many centuries after his time.

The Hebrew Bible is actually written in two closely related languages: Hebrew and Aramaic. It is called the *Hebrew Bible*, though, because only small portions are written in Aramaic: Daniel 2:4–7:28; Ezra 4:8–6:18; 7:12–26; Jeremiah 10:11; and two words in Genesis 31:47.

Now that we have a better appreciation for what is meant by "Hebrew Bible," let us now consider the term "Masoretic." This word is the adjectival form of the noun "Masorah," which in simple terms is a system of quality control used by a group of medieval Jewish scribes to ensure that the Hebrew Bible was transmitted accurately according to the tradition that they inherited. These scribes are known as the "Masoretes." The term "Masorah" is often understood to come from a Hebrew word family whose basic meaning is "to pass on a tradition."[1] But regardless of the word's etymology, the Masoretes made it their work to pass on the textual tradition that they had received, despite its shortcomings.

There were three masoretic traditions—the Babylonian, Palestinian, and Tiberian—all of which date to the last centuries of the first millennium CE.[2] It is the Tiberian tradition, which

---

[1] For a survey of the various explanation of the term "Masorah," see Yeivin, *Introduction to the Tiberian Masorah*, 34-35.

[2] A number of manuscripts are the product of the cross-pollination of masoretic traditions. One such example is the Jewish Theological Seminary's manuscript "N," for a discussion of which see Weiss, "The Masorah of The

was centered in the city of Tiberias, a city on the western shore of the Sea of Galilee, that was recognized early on as superior to the others,[3] and it is the only one of the three traditions known to have produced a full Bible.[4] The Tiberian Masoretes, which flourished from the eighth to tenth centuries CE, quickly gained ascendency, and it is the Tiberian Hebrew Bible of the Ben Asher school that is the Hebrew Bible that is used by most today. It is no surprise, then, that it was the Tiberian Masoretic Bible that became the basis for modern scholarly editions of the Hebrew Bible as well as modern English translations.

The Masorah

Generally, the term Masorah is used by Hebrew Bible scholars in a very narrow sense to refer to scribal notes added to biblical manuscripts to help ensure the correct transmission of the sacred texts.[5] Synagogue scrolls only include the consonantal text, because this is all that was permitted since early rabbinic times, when strict rules for the copying of the texts were established. As we noted above, the "Masorah" was developed in the Middle Ages to help ensure the accurate transmission of the received text. The Masoretic additions to the Hebrew Bible's

---

Jewish Theological Seminary of America Library Manuscript 232 (E. N. Adler Ms. 346)," 120-22. Weiss also notes that even the "Crown" of the Tiberian tradition, the Aleppo Codex, shows some non-Tiberian influence.

[3]   Ofer, "The History and Authority of the Aleppo Codex," 27.

[4]   Barthélemy, *Studies in the Text of the Old Testament: An Introduction to the Hebrew Old Testament Text Project*, 274-75.

[5]   See the discussion of "Masorah parva" and "Masorah magna" below.

Figure 1: A page from the Leningrad Codex containing Exodus 19:13b-20:15a.

consonantal text include vowel marks, diacritical marks, and cantillation marks, which serve—in part—to identify stress and punctuation. The Masorah also includes in the margins to the left and right of the biblical text short notations written in Aramaic that concern a number of issues relating to the biblical text, including orthography (i.e., spelling conventions), grammar, pronunciation, meaning, and cantillation. These notes are referred to as the Masorah parva (Heb. *masorah qetanah*), which means "small Masorah." The longer notes in the header and footer of the page are known as the Masorah magna (Heb.

masorah gedolah), which means "big Masorah." The Masorah magna notes are lengthier because they expound matters that the Masorah parva addresses only in brief.[6] Figure 1 is a folio or page from the eleventh-century Leningrad Codex, the text presented in the most commonly used scholarly editions of the Hebrew Bible. The three columns that occupy the center of the page consist of the biblical text, to which vowel, cantillation, and diacritical marks are added. In the margins and footers are the Masorah parva and the Masorah magna, respectively.

The first line of text in figure 1, located in the top-right corner of the folio, is בְּהֵמָה אִם־אִישׁ לֹא יִחְיֶה.[7] This text looks very different in synagogue manuscripts, because they do not contain any of the masoretic elements: בהמה אם איש לא יחיה. Without the help of the masoretic additions, one is more likely to encounter difficulty in pronunciation, accentuation, and the proper division of the text into words, phrases, and sentences.

Masoretic rules may not have been written down until the seventh century,[8] but it is clear from talmudic evidence that they were not created out of whole cloth. According to one passage in the Babylonian Talmud, God delivered to Moses at Sinai not only the proto-Masoretic text, but the pronunciation and spelling of written and read traditions (such as the *qeri/ketiv*).[9] And this rabbinic tradition persisted throughout the Middle Ages, as we can see from the systematic refutation of this position by sixteenth-century masoretic scholar Elijah Ben

---

[6]   Space constraints do not permit us to fully explore the Masorah. Readers who wish to acquire a more comprehensive understanding of the Masorah are encouraged to see Martín Contreras, "Masora and Masoretic Interpretation;" Dotan, "Masorah;" Khan, *A Short Introduction to the Tiberian Masoretic Bible and its Reading Tradition* (2nd ed.).

[7]   Remember, Hebrew reads right to left!

[8]   Dotan suggests that it was likely not until the codex gained traction in Judaism around the sixth or seventh century CE that the matters with which the Masoretes would become preoccupied could be written down (Dotan, "Masorah," 609).

[9]   B. Nezikin 37b-38a.

Asher, who is better known as Elias Levita. Concerning the origin of the vowels, pointing, and cantillation, he writes:

> Having now reached the place in which I, at the beginning of this Introduction, promised to state my own opinion about the points and accents, I shall first do battle against those who say that they were given on Sinai, and then state who invented them, and when they were originated and affixed to the letters. But if anyone should prove to me, by clear evidence, that my opinion is opposed to that of our Rabbins of blessed memory, or is contrary to the genuine Kabbalah of the *Sohar*, I will readily give in to him, and declare my opinion as void. Up to this time, however, I have neither found, nor seen, nor heard, any evidence, nor anything approaching to it, that is worthy to be relied upon, that the points and accents were given upon Sinai.[10]

From the discussion that follows it is clear that this was a matter of some doctrinal importance and a source of religious contention. In the intervening centuries, discoveries of Hebrew documents from the first millennium BCE through the masoretic period confirm that Elijah Ben Asher was indeed correct; the vowel signs, the diacritical marks, and the accents signs that accompany the consonantal Hebrew text in masoretic manuscripts are indeed the innovation of the Masoretes, and they created these signs in order to preserve a reading tradition that they had inherited. This was necessary because the rabbis did not always agree on how a text should be read. One such instance is found in Isaiah 9:19. The word that the Masoretic text reads as "his arm" (Heb. *zero'o*) was, according to Raba, to be read as "his seed" (Heb. *zar'o*).[11] While the two words sound significantly different, they are written identically in Hebrew: זרעו. The Masoretes, then, in adding these signs to the biblical text were actually transmitting an *interpreted* biblical text.

---

[10] Ben Asher & Ginsburg, *The Massoreth ha-Massoreth of Elias Levita*, 121.

[11] B. Shab. 33a.

Let us now direct our attention back to the Masorah parva and the Masorah magna. To indicate the word or phrase in the Hebrew text with which the marginal Masorah parva note is concerned, the Masoretes placed a small circle (often called a "circule" or a "circellus") above the word or phrase in question. In figure 2, the marginal note בֹ belongs to the form וְהִנְּכֶם (Deuteronomy 1:10) because of the circellus that is over the

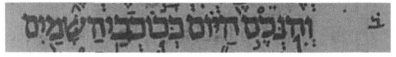

Figure 2: A portion of Deuteronomy 1:10 from the Leningrad Codex containing the Masorah parva note בֹ.

fourth letter of the word: כ. Because ב is the second letter of the Hebrew alphabet, this note means that וְהִנְּכֶם occurs a total of two times in the Hebrew Bible. Many of the most common Masorah parva notes, like this one, are simply numbers. This is because the Masoretes concern themselves with counting the exact number of various Hebrew words and phrases. As I indicated above, however, many notes are concerned with the correct spelling, cantillation mark(s), and even the proper order of words in a phrase. Some notes even deal with word meaning, as is the case with the note for "portion" (Heb. *wehevel*) in Joshua 17:14.[12]

For the purpose of this book, one particularly important type of Masorah parva note is the *qeri/ketiv*, which we have already addressed briefly above. The term *qeri*[13] is Aramaic for "It is read," while the term *ketiv* means "It is written." These two terms are used together to describe a phenomenon in which the biblical text presents one reading in the text itself—the *ketiv*—while another is presented in the margin – the *qeri*.[14] While the

---

[12]   Dotan, *The Awakening of Word Lore: From the Masora to the Beginnings of Hebrew Lexicography*, 78; Dost, *The Sub-Loco Notes in the Former Prophets*, 42.
[13]   Sometimes spelled "*qere*."
[14]   For a detailed explanation, Martín-Contreras, "Ketib/Qere," 145-47; M. Cohen, *The Kethib and Qeri System in the Biblical Text: A Linguistic*

origins and reasons for this phenomenon are debated, many instances of *qeri/ketiv* bear witness to a certain amount of textual fluidity that still existed in the masoretic period.[15] And the Babylonian Talmud contains evidence of an orally transmitted pre-masoretic reading tradition according to which certain words were pronounced differently from the way that they were eventually recorded in the Masoretic text.[16] For example, the Leningrad Codex says that "Abraham set up *his* tent (אָהֳלֹה, *'oholo*)." Without the vowel marks, however, the consonantal text אהלה can also be read as "*her* tent" (*'ohola*), which is the reading followed in the Talmud.[17] In some cases, a *qeri* is found without a corresponding *ketiv*, as is the case in Ruth 3:5. The text that is printed should be translated, "And she said

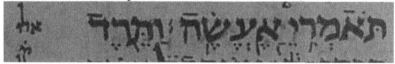

Figure 3: Between the words תֹּאמְרִי ("you say") and אֶעֱשֶׂה ("I will do") is inserted a circellus which draws the reader's attention to the marginal note אלי ק ("It is read: 'to me'").

to her, 'I will do all that you say.'" If one follows the *qeri*, however, one must translate, "And she said to her, 'I will do all that you say *to me*'" (see figure 3).

As we have noted above, the Masorah magna often presents in detail what is stated concisely and somewhat cryptically in a Masorah parva note. For example, in the Leningrad Codex the Hebrew form לְכָה in Isaiah 3:6 is given the Masorah parva note ד מל ("Four times with full spelling").[18] In the lower-right margin of the page is a much longer Masorah

---

Analysis of the Various Traditions Based on the Manuscript "Keter Aram Tsova," 1.

[15] For a *qeri/ketiv* that presents a fundamentally different reading, see Dost, *The Sub-Loco Notes*, 21

[16] B. Sanhedrin 4a.

[17] B. Yebamot 62b.

[18] The sense of this note is "This word occurs four times with full (= longer) spelling."

magna note that gives the four occurrences with full or longer spelling and the three additional occurrences that have defective or shorter spelling.[19]

Is the Tiberian Masoretic Bible Reliable?

Virtually all students of the Hebrew Bible work exclusively with the Tiberian Masoretic text. In fact, all of the standard biblical Hebrew grammars teach Hebrew from the text of the Leningrad Codex because it serves as the basis for the most commonly used scholarly edition, *Biblia Hebraica Stuttgartensia* (*BHS*).[20] The Leningrad Codex is the oldest *complete* manuscript of the entire Hebrew Bible (ca. 1008 CE), and it is a very reliable witness to the Tiberian Hebrew reading tradition of the famed Ben Asher school. As a Tiberian witness, however, the Leningrad Codex has its faults.

The crowning achievement of the Tiberian Masoretic school is the Aleppo Codex, which dates to ca. 950 CE.[21] Shlomo Ben Buya'a produced the biblical text, and Aharon Ben Asher was the text's Masorete and vocalizer. The Aleppo Codex is hands down the most reliable Tiberian Masoretic manuscript. Within the entire corpus of the Prophets, for instance, the Aleppo Codex only contradicts the Masorah twice.[22] The Cairo and Leningrad codices are the second and third best Tiberian manuscripts of the Prophets, containing 130 and 280 errors, respectively.[23] Unfortunately, as I note elsewhere:[24]

---

[19]   See Dost, *The Sub-Loco Notes*, 87. In some of these Masorah magna lists the Masoretes display their "scribal wit," as David Marcus puts it, by creating Aramaic mnemonics to aid in the memorization of the lists' contents (Marcus, *Scribal Wit,* 157).

[20]   The German Bible Society is currently producing a new scholarly edition, *Biblia Hebraica Quinta* (*BHQ*), which will replace *BHS*.

[21]   Ofer, "The History and Authority of the Aleppo Codex," 25.

[22]   Breuer, *The Biblical Text*, א-י.

[23]   Dost, *The Sub-Loco Notes*, 8.

[24]   Ibid., 4.

...many folios of the Aleppo Codex have been lost, whether because they were removed sometime before the manuscript arrived in Israel,[25] consumed by fire during the Syrian riots of 1947,[26] or destroyed by fungi.[27]

Masoretic research has allowed scholars to produce a reliable reconstruction of the text of the Aleppo Codex, however, which is published under the editorship of Menachem Cohen in *Mikra'ot Gedolot 'Haketer.* '[28]

The Tiberian Masoretes accomplished a great feat by producing and applying their extensive system of quality control to the Hebrew Bible. We must remember, though, that they did not preserve the *best* text; they merely did *their* best to preserve the text tradition that they inherited.[29] Given our space constraints, we cannot even scratch the surface of the topic of the corruption of the Masoretic text tradition. The following examples illustrate only a few types of textual corruption,[30] but they are more than adequate to illustrate the point that the Masoretic text tradition is not a perfect text.

The first type of corruption that we shall examine concerns incorrect word division. There are instances in the Hebrew Bible in which the consonantal text is correct, but the word division is not. One such example occurs in Amos 6:12. According to the three best Tiberian manuscripts of the Prophets—the Aleppo, Leningrad, and Cairo codices—the first

---

[25]   Ofer, "The History and Authority of the Aleppo Codex," 30. For a more detailed treatment of the history of the Aleppo Codex from the 1947 pogrom in Aleppo until the manuscript's arrival in Israel in 1958, see Tawil and Schneider, *Crown of Aleppo: The Mystery of the Oldest Hebrew Bible Codex*, 75–106. For a new perspective on the fate of the Aleppo Codex in the wake of the Syrian riots, see Friedman, *The Aleppo Codex*.

[26]   Ofer, "The History and Authority of the Aleppo Codex," 29.

[27]   See Polachek et al., "Damage to an Ancient Parchment Document by Aspergillus," 89–93.

[28]   See Ofer, "The History and Authority of the Aleppo Codex," 40–43.

[29]   Marcus & Sanders, "What's Critical about a Critical Edition of the Bible?" 62.

[30]   For a detailed treatment, see Tov, *TCHB*[3], 219-62.

half of the verse should be translated, "Do horses run on rocks? Does one plow with oxen?" It is clear from the context that both statements were meant to be rhetorical questions that demand a negative reply. Horses clearly do not run on rocks, but ploughing is done with oxen. If one follows the text as it stands, the logic of the passage is lost. If, however, one divides the Hebrew word בבקרים "with oxen" into two words בבקר ים, the resulting translation of the second question is "Does one plough the sea with oxen?" which has far greater correspondence to "Do horses run on rocks?"

Sometimes, textual corruptions result in humorous readings. One such example occurs in 1 Samuel 13:1. The reading found in the three aforementioned Tiberian codices produces the following translation:

Saul was one year old when he began to reign, and he reigned over Israel for two years.

If ever there were a verse that demonstrates the errancy of the Masoretic text, this is it! Targum Jonathan (ca. fourth century CE) attempts to rescue the text by treating the phrase "one year old" metaphorically:

Saul was like a one year old in whom there is no guilt when he began to reign, and he reigned over Israel for two years.

While Targum Jonathan's interpretation is quite clever, there is no doubt that the Hebrew text is corrupt.

There are instances of premeditated textual corruption, too. One such example is the deliberate corruption of personal names containing the divine name "Baal." For example, in 2 Samuel 11:21 the Masoretic text mentions the name "Jerubbesheth" (ירבשת). We know, however, from the Greek version of 2 Samuel 11:21 and other verses within the Masoretic text that the name is "Jerubaal" (ירבעל), a name which is attested in the biblical period.[31] By changing the last two letters of the name, "May Baal contend" was transformed to "May Shame contend," which, as Emanuel Tov contends, was done to counter polytheistic belief.[32]

A far more striking anti-polytheistic alteration occurs in the Masoretic Text of Deuteronomy 32:8. According to this textual tradition, verses 8-9 can be translated:

[8]*When the Most-High apportioned the nations, when he divided the children of man, he established the boundaries of the nations according to the number of the sons of Israel.* [9]*For Yahweh's*[33] *portion is his people; Jacob is his allotted inheritance.*

According to this reading, "the Most-High" appears to be Yahweh, Israel's God. Much as in Genesis 10, Yahweh is presented as Lord over all. There is a certain awkwardness in the text, however, which requires some explanation. If Israel's God is indeed the Most-High, why does he divide the world into twelve nations? If his sole interest is in Israel, it makes little sense to divide all others into eleven groups. When we look at a manuscript of Deuteronomy that was discovered among the Dead Sea Scrolls (4Q37), we find a more difficult and more authentic reading:

---

[31] Tigay, *You Shall Have No Other Gods: Israelite Religion in the Light of Hebrew Inscriptions*, 68-69.

[32] Tov, *TCHB³*, 247-48. It is also very clearly the case with "Merodach" in Jer 50:2. The actual name of the god to whom the text refers is "Marduk," who was the chief god of Babylon.

[33] It has long been customary within Judaism to substitute God's personal name Yahweh with "the Lord" so as not to take "His name in vain." Gordis argues from biblical and extrabiblical evidence that this practice was well established by the third century BCE (Gordis, *The Biblical Text in the Making: A Study of the Kethib-Qere*, 29-30). I break with that tradition here only because this particular textual issue requires us to be specific about the divine names.

>*When the Most-High apportioned the nations, when he divided the children of man, he established the boundaries of the nations according to the number of the sons of God. *For Yahweh's portion is His people; Jacob is his allotted inheritance.*

This reading, which seems to distinguish between Yahweh and the Most-High, reflects a notion that characterized ancient Israel thought for much of its history, namely, that Yahweh, its god, was not the chief god of the pantheon. As Canaanite texts indicate, that place is occupied by El-Elyon ("God Most High").[34] Yahweh would have been a second-tier, national deity, on par with other national deities. While this may sound strange to some readers, there are many other passages in the Hebrew Bible that reflect this idea, most notably Psalm 82, and perhaps even the command to have no other gods before Yahweh (Exodus 20:2-3). It is Ezekiel's aim in chapter ten to abrogate this ancient Near Eastern idea of a hierarchy of gods and goddesses, which would have been quite at home in ancient Israel.[35] The fully Canaanite pantheon did eventually collapse over the course of ancient Israelite history, resulting in Yahweh's slow rise to the top of the pantheon and eventually to sole, universal God, as he is depicted in Daniel 7.[36] The reason for providing all of these examples, though, is not to digress into a discussion of ancient historical theology but rather to show that the Masoretic Text tradition is not as neat and tidy as some readers would expect it to be or hope it to be.

Conclusion

The proto-Masoretic text was one of at least three distinct biblical text traditions in circulation during the late Second Temple period. This textual tradition from which the Masoretes

---

[34]   See M. Smith, *The Origins of Biblical Monotheism*, 41-46.
[35]   See 2 Kings 3, especially verses 26-27.
[36]   See M. Smith, *The Origins of Biblical Monotheism*, 47-53.

would work, became the *textus receptus* (Lat., "received text") around the time of the two Jewish revolts against Rome (66-73 CE & 132-136 CE), when the consonantal text became largely stabilized.[37] The Tiberian Hebrew Masoretic Bible, which is *the* Hebrew Bible for most students and scholars today, has as its foundation a partially corrupt, imperfectly transmitted text from Jesus' day. But though this textual tradition is regarded as authoritative today for many Jews and Christians, it should not be assumed to be the best version of the Hebrew Bible; and it certainly does not preserve the "original text" of any biblical book, as leading textual critic Emanuel Tov emphatically warns.[38]

While the Masoretes believed in a very literal sense that "one jot or one tittle (should) in no wise pass from the law,"[39] the fact is that far more than jots and tittles were added to and subtracted from biblical manuscripts over the course of the biblical text's transmission history. This does not mean that the text that we read today bears no resemblance to the text that Jesus read in the synagogue. That is the farthest thing from the truth.

As I stated earlier, our goal here is not to debate theology. I recognize, however, that many readers are interested in considering how the foregoing may impact one theological view of Scripture or another. For this reason, it may be worth noting that the patristic and medieval Church was aware of these textual problems. But as Brogan observes, the early Church did not regard the manuscripts' textual problems as impediments to the faithful transmission of Scripture's message.[40] Some Christian denominations are aware of this, and their theological statements reflect it. Others, however, hold to doctrinal statements that reflect ideology and not historical reality. Seeing the Tiberian

---

[37] Barthélemy, *Studies in the Text of the Old Testament*, 276.
[38] Tov, *TCHB*[3], 11-12.
[39] Matthew 5:18.
[40] John J. Brogan, "Can I Have Your Autograph? Uses and Abuses of Textual Criticism in Formulating an Evangelical Doctrine of Scripture," 95.

Masoretic Hebrew Bible for what it is, we are forced to come to grips with the fact that the Hebrew text that we use or which we encounter indirectly through translations is *textually imperfect*. And while this may force readers into the uncomfortable position of having to reassess their theology of Scripture, such reflection is necessary for a meaningful twenty-first century dialogue of faith and reason.[41]

***

So far, we have painted with broad strokes a picture of the final form of the Hebrew Bible, the Tiberian Masoretic Hebrew Bible (henceforth, "the Masoretic Text").[42] As we noted, this Bible was not in existence in Jesus' day. In fact, there was no Hebrew Bible, just sacred texts circulating on scrolls, only some of which would become part of the Jewish Bible or become part of one of the Christian Old Testament canons. In order to understand how this state of affairs developed, we need to trace the development of the biblical texts from their inception onward. This is a difficult task, however, because the earliest preserved manuscripts of many of these texts date from over half a millennium after the first contributors put the proverbial pen to paper.

Given this lack of evidence, how do scholars recover the history of these documents? In short, we look for the clues that the authors and redactors/editors deliberately and inadvertently incorporated into their work. As these countless individuals wrote, copied, and developed these texts, they, as all writers do, brought their world into the text. The biblical texts were written in their language, with constant reference to their geography, culture, and history. All such evidence, when taken together, allows scholars to determine with varying degrees of certainty

---

[41] For further discussion see Brogan, "Can I Have Your Autograph?" 109.
[42] Use of this term is scholarly convention, and we use it here merely for convenience's sake.

where, when, why, and by whom the individual biblical texts were written.

In the next four chapters, we shall look at the four aforementioned types of evidence that aid scholars in their investigation of the Hebrew Bible's historical development. In chapter 2, we will briefly examine the clues in the very language of the texts themselves, examining how various features of the languages (e.g., vocabulary, spelling conventions, grammar, and syntax) can impact our understanding of the development of the Hebrew Bible. The subsequent three chapters deal with the problems of (1) reading the Hebrew Bible as ancient historiography, (2) reading it in the light of ancient Near Eastern literature, and (3) reading the biblical texts as ancient "books." At that point, we will be ready to better answer the question, Who wrote the Bible?

2
BIBLICAL HEBREW

The Hebrew Language: Its History[1]

Biblical Hebrew is not a uniform language. This may come as a surprise to many readers who have studied a year or two of Hebrew in college or graduate school, because the history of Hebrew is rarely addressed in such classes. The language developed through various phases during the "biblical period," the roughly one-thousand-year span during which the Hebrew Bible was composed and redacted. Scholars see three to four distinct phases of Hebrew within the biblical record itself. A four-phase approach divides biblical Hebrew into the following groups: (1) Archaic or Old, (2) Standard or Classical, (3) Transitional, and (4) Late.[2]

Given the traditional belief that Moses wrote the Pentateuch, it may come as a surprise to some that there are very few texts within the Hebrew Bible that are categorized as Archaic Biblical Hebrew (ABH). There are ten texts that are generally assigned to this phase of Biblical Hebrew. I present them in order of their appearance in the Jewish Bible.

---

[1] We shall not get into the details of historical Hebrew grammar, as introductory books such as this one are not the appropriate place to discuss such technical matters, nor do I assume that many of those reading this have had the requisite training in Hebrew to benefit from such information. A few of the works referenced in this book that will benefit those wishing to explore historical Hebrew grammar are Blau, *Phonology and Morphology of Biblical Hebrew*; Schniedewind, *A Social History of Hebrew: Its Origins Through the Rabbinic Period*; Garr and Fassberg, *A Handbook of Biblical Hebrew: Volume 1: Periods, Corpora, and Reading Traditions*.

[2] Lam and Pardee, "Standard/Classical Biblical Hebrew," 1; and it is principally upon this work that the following description of the four phases of biblical Hebrew is based. Other scholars employ a simpler, three-phase structure: Archaic, Standard, and Late (see, e.g., Kutscher, *A History of the Hebrew Language*, 12; Schniedewind, *A Social History of Hebrew*, 6).

1. Genesis 49:2-27
2. Exodus 15:1-18
3. Numbers 23:7-10; 23:18-24; 24:3-9; 24:16-19
4. Deuteronomy 32:1-43
5. Deuteronomy 33:1-29
6. Judges 5:1-30
7. 1 Samuel 2:1-10
8. 2 Samuel 22:2-51 (= Psalm 18)
9. Habakkuk 3
10. Psalm 68

However, because there is so little evidence with which to work, it is difficult to differentiate between truly archaic Hebrew forms and forms that are less common and dialectical, in part because many of the characteristics of ABH are found in the second phase, Standard Biblical Hebrew (SBH). This has led some to regard ABH as a distinct style of Hebrew and not necessarily an earlier phase.[3] This ambiguity means that we cannot assume that these texts are necessarily older than the corpus of SBH texts. Furthermore, it means that we cannot assume that these texts necessarily shed light on the way in which Hebrew was spoken in a given city or region in the periods in which the ABH texts are set.[4]

Spoken Hebrew differed from region to region (if not village to village) partly because even in its earliest days, Israel interacted with various polities and often exchanged control of territories with those who spoke a different form of the language or another Semitic language altogether. We get a small glimpse into the complexity of early Hebrew in Judges 12:5-6:

> *Gilead captured the fords of the Jordan against Ephraim.*
> *Now when one of the fugitives of Ephraim would say, "Let me*
> *pass," the men of Gilead would say to him, "You are*

---

[3] Young, *Diversity in Pre-Exilic Hebrew*, 123.
[4] Gianto, "Archaic Biblical Hebrew," 19. On orthography (spelling conventions) as an unreliable guide to pronunciation, see Schniedewind, *A Social History of Hebrew*, 10-12.

Ephraimite." But he would say, "No." So they would say to him, "Say, 'Shibboleth.'" But he would say, "Sibboleth." For he could not pronounce this. So they would take him and slay him at the fords of the Jordan. And from Ephraim there fell at that time 42,000.

We learn from this passage that even in nearby regions, a person's place of origin was immediately evident from his or her pronunciation of Hebrew.[5] The same is true with modern Palestinian Arabic. In villages that are a short car ride from one another certain words are pronounced differently, and in some cases the pronunciation characteristic of one village is almost unintelligible to those who live a village away.[6] But the point that I want to establish is that Hebrew, like English, evolved over time, and that process did not happen uniformly, which has led scholars to present significantly different dates for certain portions of the Hebrew Bible. This issue is further complicated by the fact that precise vowel markers were not added to the biblical text until the masoretic period (as we saw in chapter 1), which means that one cannot fully and confidently determine to what degree the pronunciation preserved in the Masoretic Text reflects the pronunciation of Hebrew at the time when and in the place where a given text was written.[7]

Traditionally, "Standard Biblical Hebrew" has been used to describe the predominant style of Genesis through 2 Kings, but a number of poetical texts, too, despite their use of archaic

---

[5] Likewise, many Israelis who grow up speaking Hebrew and Arabic cannot completely disguise which language they speak at home.

[6] Somewhat analogously, most who grow up in Long Island or in Boston cannot conceal their place of origin from someone who grew up in, say, Connecticut. Having grown up in Connecticut myself, I always found it amusing that when my grandmother from Foxboro, Massachusetts, talked about an "idea," the sound "r" somehow found its way onto the end of the word; yet when it was time for "dinner," the sound "r" was nowhere to be found.

[7] Hornkohl, "Transitional Biblical Hebrew," 37.

forms, belong to this phase as well.[8] Despite the fact that SBH texts were redacted during and even after the Babylonian Exile of the sixth century BCE, SBH is generally considered a predominantly pre-exilic layer of biblical Hebrew.

Transitional Biblical Hebrew (TBH) has been considered to extend from roughly the end of the First Temple period (586 BCE) through the early Second Temple period (ca. 450 BCE).[9] According to Hornkohl, the texts that form the TBH corpus are Isaiah 40-66; Jeremiah; Ezekiel; Haggai; Zechariah; Malachi; Lamentations; 2 Kings 24-25.[10]

The corpus of Late Biblical Hebrew (LBH) texts includes those works that were composed later in the Second Temple period. The general consensus is that the LBH corpus includes Ecclesiastes, Esther, Daniel, Ezra-Nehemiah, and Chronicles, though some would add Song of Songs, Jonah, and certain psalms.[11] Copies of many of them are preserved among the Dead Sea Scrolls, which provides the latest possible date of their composition. Among the LBH works preserved in the Dead Sea Scrolls are Ezra-Nehemiah, Chronicles, Ecclesiastes, and Daniel. The one LBH work not preserved at Qumran is Esther.[12]

Not all scholars agree that all of the aforementioned LBH texts should actually be categorized as LBH, however. It was customary in twentieth-century biblical scholarship to regard texts that contained Aramaic words as late. Song of Songs and Ecclesiastes, for example, were generally considered to be late, even though they were traditionally understood to have been authored by the great tenth-century BCE king Solomon, because of their use of "Aramaisms." To be sure, there is good reason to

---

8   Lam and Pardee, "Standard/Classical Biblical Hebrew," 2.
9   Hornkohl, "Transitional Biblical Hebrew," 31-32.
10   Ibid. 32-33.
11   Morgenstern, "Late Biblical Hebrew," 44-45. For a discussion of an early date for Song of Songs, see, for example, Young, *Diversity in Pre-Exilic Hebrew*, 157-65; Noegel and Rendsburg, *Solomon's Vineyard: Literary and Linguistic Studies in the Song of Solomon*, 174-84.
12   For an explanation as to why this is the case, see Talmon, "Was the Book of Esther Known At Qumran?"

consider the presence of Aramaic words in Hebrew texts as indicating lateness, because when the people of Judah (the Israelites who lived in and around Jerusalem) were exiled to Babylon in 586 BCE, Aramaic was the spoken language there.[13] And as one can see from Ezra 4:7, Aramaic was often used for international correspondence in the subsequent Achaemenid (or Persian) period.[14] So it is quite natural to assume that many if not most of the native Hebrew speakers and their descendants who lived in Babylonia during the sixth century onward would have not only spoken Aramaic[15] but would have intentionally and unintentionally used Aramaic words even when they were speaking and writing Hebrew.

Yet, as compelling as the argument may be, it is important to note that the people of Israel were interacting with Aramaic speakers long before the Babylonian exile. The oldest extant Aramaic documents date back to the end of the tenth century BCE,[16] a time when the northern kingdom of Israel had regular interaction with their Aramaic-speaking neighbors to the north, the Arameans.[17] According to 2 Samuel 8:5-6, David, the tenth-century Israelite king, subjugated the Arameans, which, if historically reliable, means Aramaic and Hebrew speakers had come into contact by this time.[18] By the ninth century there existed at least one document written in Aramaic that mentions

---

[13] Foster and Foster, *Civilizations of Ancient Iraq*, 137.

[14] "Now in the days of Artaxerxes, Bishlam, Mithredath, Tabeel, and the rest of their colleagues wrote to Artaxerxes, the king of Persia, and the letter was written in Aramaic and was translated."

[15] Bottéro, Herrenschmidt, and Vernant, *Ancestors of the West: Writing, Reasoning, and Religion in Mesopotamia, Elam, and Greece*, 17.

[16] Rubin, *A Brief Introduction to the Semitic Languages*, 18; *KAI*, 2.203.

[17] Some translations refer to this people group as the "Syrians," because the territory that was ancient Aram largely overlaps with modern Syria.

[18] Some scholars express skepticism concerning the historicity of biblical narratives set in the tenth century, though the tide is turning. We shall address this in the next chapter.

the defeat of "the king of Israel" and "[the king of] the house of David" at the hands of the king of Aram.[19] Aramaic had already been spoken in Mesopotamia since around the turn of the first millennium BCE,[20] and the Assyrian empire was known to have communicated in Aramaic, as 2 Kings 18:26 (= Isaiah 36:11) indicates.[21] It can safely be said, therefore, that Aramaic was known at least by those in power in Israel from the tenth century onward, which means that Aramaisms were likely part of the Hebrew language during the entirety of the monarchical period, if not before. In fact, a number of leading Hebrew scholars believe that the Hebrew of northern Israel, the part of the country closer to Aram, was naturally more akin to Aramaic than the Hebrew of Jerusalem. It is not surprising, then, that recent research has argued that many of the compositions that were formerly regarded as late are quite possibly pre-exilic (i.e., written before the Babylonian Exile of 586 BCE) and written in northern, Israelian Hebrew or in "an Aramaizing dialect."[22]

Therefore, one may not determine that a biblical text was written later in Israel's history only on the basis of Aramaisms. In fact, one may not date a text to any period, early or late, without examining a number of other factors. In the next chapter, we shall explore how historical references and allusions in biblical texts can help to more accurately determine a text's date.

---

[19] For a transcription and translation of the text with commentary, see Aḥituv, *Echoes from the Past*, 466-73.

[20] Akkadian-Aramaic bilingual compositions date to as early as the ninth century BCE, and by the eight century BCE, Aramaisms are found in Akkadian texts (Kuhrt, *The Ancient Near East c. 3000-330 BC*, 397-398).

[21] "Then Eliakim son of Hilkiah, Shebna, and Joah said to Rabshakeh, 'Speak to your servants in Aramaic, for we understand it. But do not speak with us in Judahite (i.e., Hebrew) in the ears of the people who are on the wall.'"

[22] Noegel and Rendsburg, *Solomon's Vineyard*, 5.

3
ISRAEL & JUDAH'S PAST:
HISTORY & HISTORIOGRAPHY

"The conceptions of history have been almost as numerous
as the men who have written history."
                                    –Fredrick Jackson Turner[1]

The Hebrew Bible was penned over the course of the first
millennium BCE in what is known today as the Middle East.
Many of the biblical texts were written in Israel and Judah
(roughly modern-day Israel and Palestine), while others were
written in Babylonia (southeastern Iraq) and in Egypt. The first
millennium was an age of empire. The Israelites and Judeans,
the ancestors of the Jews (if I may oversimplify matters for the
present), lived under foreign domination or under the threat
thereof for most of their history, and we cannot overstate how
significantly foreign domination impacted the growth,
development, and interpretation of the Hebrew Scriptures.

While the Hebrew Bible was written in the first
millennium BCE, the setting of the biblical story extends all the
way back to "the beginning."[2] The first eleven chapters of the

---

[1]   Fredrick Jackson Turner, "The Significance of History," 230.
[2]   It is worth noting that most English translations mistranslate the
Hebrew of Genesis 1:1-2. Many English translations follow the KJV, which
translates the Hebrew with "In the beginning God created the heaven and the
earth. And the earth was without form, and void; and darkness was upon the
face of the deep. And the Spirit of God moved upon the face of the waters."
A better translation is "When God began to create the heavens and the earth,
the earth was without form and void and darkness was upon the face of the
deep, while the spirit of God hovered over the face of the waters." This latter
and more accurate rendering of the Hebrew conveys that when God began to
create, he did not start from scratch. There was already a water-world. This

book of Genesis, which are commonly known as the "Primeval History," take the reader on a journey that includes the creation of the cosmos, the propagation of humanity, a world-wide flood, and the dispersion of humanity from Babylon (Hebrew *bavel*, or, as it is commonly rendered, *Babel*).

It is at that point that God makes a promise to a Mesopotamian man named Abram (whose name is later changed to Abraham) to give to him descendants, land for his descendants, and prosperity. The remainder of Genesis (chapters 12-50) recounts how Abraham and his aged wife Sarah miraculously produce a son of their own, Isaac. It is Isaac's son Jacob (later named Israel) who becomes the father of twelve sons, the ancestors of the twelve tribes of Israel. The remainder of the Torah (Exodus, Leviticus, Numbers, and Deuteronomy) and the Former Prophets (Joshua, Judges, Samuel, and Kings) tell the story of how the family of Jacob's descendants fled oppression in Egypt under their God-ordained leader Moses, received God's Instruction, conquered the land of Canaan, and became a united kingdom under David. As Kings records, however, David's united monarchy was not to last. Under the watch of his grandson Rehoboam, the kingdom was divided into two: Israel in the north and Judah in the south. These two kingdoms were eventually conquered and exiled by the Assyrians (721 BCE) and the Babylonians (586 BCE), respectively, after which some returned to rebuild Jerusalem and its temple to the God of Israel.

This, in a nutshell, is the story of the Hebrew Bible. Traditionally, the biblical texts that tell this story have been understood as historically reliable accounts of Israel's past, and this is a matter of some consequence. For many, aspects of their worldview[3]—whether it be the notion that humanity was created

---

means that one should speak of Genesis 1:1 as "the beginning" only in a qualified sense.

[3] Simply put, a worldview is one's answers to ultimate questions, which address life's meaning, purpose, and significance. For further

by God or the belief that God bequeathed to them a certain land where they and their descendants may live and fulfill God's decrees—rest upon the assumption that the Hebrew Bible's accounts of the past are historically reliable.

Though many faith communities come to the Hebrew Scriptures with the presupposition that they are very reliable or even completely reliable, most biblical scholars do not share this perspective. One reason for this is that many details, statements, and stories simply cannot be proven. Take, for instance, 2 Kings 19:35, a passage in which God sends his angel to slay 185,000 Assyrians in order to save Hezekiah and Jerusalem. During a discussion of this text in a history seminar, one of my graduate school professors stated bluntly: In biblical scholarship, there is no such thing as miracle. What he meant by this is that biblical scholarship draws conclusions from available evidence. It is not possible for anyone to prove that the miracle recounted in 2 Kings 19:35 actually happened; that is a matter of faith. Because of the nature of their craft, most biblical scholars do not assume stories of miracle to be true.[4] This is because most biblical scholars are historians, and historians deal with the empirical, that which is observable. In building conclusions, historians deal with facts, not faith. In an effort to be as scientific as possible in their research of the past, they gather data from texts and physical artifacts, which they then interpret. For the historian, stories about the slaying of 185,000 Assyrians by an angel is not supported by material evidence and therefore not considered historical. Likewise, the stories of Abraham (Genesis 11-25) cannot be verified or falsified by archaeology, because semi-nomadic tribal chieftains from the second millennium BCE were not in the habit of leaving behind the types of material

---

discussion, see H. Smith, *The Illustrated World's Religions: A Guide to Our Wisdom Traditions*, 10.

[4] Walton, *Ancient Near Eastern Thought and the Old Testament: Introducing the Conceptual World of the Hebrew Bible* (2d ed.), 192-93; Ehrman, *Jesus, Interrupted: Revealing the Hidden Contradictions in the Bible (and Why We Don't Known about Them)*, 172.

evidence needed by archaeologists to verify or falsify the historicity of the stories later written about them. Therefore, scholars generally do not regard these stories as historical, either.

It is true that archaeological findings (including extra-biblical texts)[5] from Israel and the ancient Near East corroborate countless statements that the Hebrew Bible makes about Israel's past.[6] Numerous Israelite and Judean monarchs are known from Mesopotamian sources. King Hezekiah is described as being "locked up within Jerusalem, his royal city, like a bird in a cage,"[7] which bears striking resemblance to the Bible's report of the Assyrian siege of Jerusalem (2 Kings 18-19; Isaiah 36-37; 2 Chronicles 32). The Tel Dan Stela,[8] a victory monument from the ninth century, makes reference to the "House of David," which, if nothing else, confirms that there was a King David who established a royal dynasty, as the Bible claims, and corroborates the Bible's claim that the Arameans were a formidable enemy of Israel in the ninth century (1 Kings 20). Another ninth-century monument, the Mesha Stela, seems to confirm the historicity of certain details of 2 Kings 3.[9] These are just three of the many examples that we could discuss here.[10]

However, there are many details within the Hebrew Bible that archaeology cannot verify for lack of evidence and many others that are contradicted by archaeological data. The story of the Exodus is notoriously problematic. There are, to be sure, several aspects of the biblical story that are at least consistent with what is known from Egyptian history.[11] From

[5]　"Extra-biblical texts" are text not included in the Bible.
[6]　For a brief discussion of the history of and developments in what is often called "biblical archaeology," see Richards, ed., *Near Eastern Archaeology: A Reader*, 33-62.
[7]　*COS* 2.119B.
[8]　*COS* 2.39.
[9]　Richelle, *The Bible and Archaeology*, 30-31.
[10]　Ibid., 75.
[11]　The following examples are drawn from Kitchen, *On the Reliability of the Old Testament*, 247-74.

Egyptian evidence we know that the Egyptians used Syrian and Canaanite foreign labor in the sixteenth to twelfth centuries BCE, and that lack of straw for making bricks was sometimes a problem (Exodus 1:9-14).[12] The book of Exodus mentions that the Hebrew slaves were responsible for building the store cities of Pithom and Ramses (Exodus 1:11). Pharaoh Ramesses II is known to have built one city, *Pi-Ramesse A-nakhtu* ("Domain of Ramesses II, Great in Victory"),[13] which is thought to be the city to which Exodus 1:11 makes reference. The city was abandoned by 1130 BCE, long before the establishment of Israel's united monarchy under King David. As for Pithom, Kitchen argues that this city is *"Pi(r)-(A)tum,* domain (lit., house) of (the god) Atum,"[14] which he identifies as Tell er-Retaba, approximately fifteen miles from the site of Pi-Ramesse. On the basis of these and other considerations, Kitchen concludes that the Exodus story is historically in touch with the period, region, and social reality that it describes.[15] After a thorough analysis of pertinent evidence, Hoffmeier likewise finds a great deal of support for the historicity of the Exodus story.[16] Some sensationalist media productions are even more affirming of the historicity of the biblical account of the Exodus,[17] but biblical scholarship is, on the whole, quite skeptical about many aspects of the account. It is difficult for many to trust the biblical account because the close of Rameses II's reign is characterized by strong borders and mining in the Sinai Peninsula[18] and with the man himself having been considered a "living legend" at the close of his

---

[12]   Ibid., 247-48.

[13]   Ibid., 255.

[14]   Ibid., 256-58.

[15]   Ibid., 311-12.

[16]   Hoffmeier, *Israel in Egypt: Evidence for the Authenticity of the Exodus Tradition*, 223-27.

[17]   See *Patterns of Evidence: The Exodus*, produced by Timothy P. Mahoney (Thinking Man Films, 2015), which highlights the work of David Rohl. This documentary aroused the stir for which it was created when it was released, but has not won acceptance by the academic community.

[18]   Van De Mieroop, *A History of Ancient Egypt*, 240, 256.

reign.[19] To many, this description of Ramesses simply does not jibe with the biblical story. For these and other reasons, some argue that the story better reflects the seventh or sixth century BCE,[20] while others argue for an even later date.[21]

Likewise, scholarship has produced a broad array of perspectives on the historicity of other biblical stories, such as the patriarchal narratives of Genesis and the book of Joshua's story of the Israelites' conquest of Canaan. The debate about the historicity of the Hebrew Bible's accounts of Abraham, Moses, and Joshua is not just fueled by the state of archaeological research. Scholars often disagree on the interpretation of individual biblical texts because they disagree on *how* historiography (i.e., writings about the past) ought to be interpreted.

History and Historiography

Before interpreting a biblical text, scholars first have to determine *how* one ought to interpret the text under consideration. This is done on a case by case basis. I find that many lay Christian Bible readers assume that if the text appears to be an historical account, that is what it must be. And because it is unthinkable to so many that the word of God could in any way contain erroneous statements about the past, these historical narratives must be completely accurate historical narratives. The Hebrew Bible, however, contains numerous passages that have caused scholars to challenge this perspective. One such example concerns the revelation of God's name. According to Exodus 6:3, God says to Moses:

---

[19]   Jacob Van Dijk, "The Amarna Period and the Later New Kingdom," 302.

[20]   Finkelstein and Mazar, *The Quest for the Historical Israel: Debating Archaeology and the History of Early Israel*, 52.

[21]   For a survey of this "minimalist" scholarship see, Dever, *What Did the Biblical Writers Know and When Did They Know It? What Archaeology Can Tell Us about the Reality of Ancient Israel*, 23-52.

*I appeared to Abraham, to Isaac, and to Jacob as El Shaddai,
but I did not disclose to them my name Yahweh.* (Exodus 6:3)

There is little doubt that God is telling Moses that his ancestors
never knew him by this name. This would appear to contradict
evidence found in Genesis, however. Eve is already familiar
with God's name Yahweh, according to Genesis 4:1. Upon the
occasion of her son Cain's birth, she exclaims that she has
produced a child "with (the help of) Yahweh." Similarly, the
words spoken by Lamech when his son Noah is born indicates
that he, too, knows God's name Yahweh.[22] Noah himself knew
God's name (Genesis 9:26). Abraham builds altars to Yahweh
(e.g., Genesis 12:7, 8), and he speaks this name when talking
with Melchizedek (Genesis 14:22). Likewise, Isaac and Jacob
both utter the divine name (Genesis 27:20, 27). These are a few
of the many examples from Genesis that reflect a tradition that
runs counter to Exodus 6:3.

What many fail to realize, however, is that in the world
of the Bible, those who wrote about the past were rarely
concerned with recording events accurately for the sake of future
generations' curiosity. The historiographers, those who wrote
about the past, usually had other, higher aims, as is the case in
many other cultures. This means that it is not safe to assume that
any particular biblical narrative is historical, in the modern sense
of the word.

Because the term "history" is commonly understood
outside of scholarship as a completely accurate account of the
past, most scholars tend to avoid using this term to categorize
biblical texts. Instead, to classify texts that "present an account
of the past," they use the term "historiography," which does not
carry the connotations that the term history bears.
"Historiography" is a more neutral term that does not imply
anything about a text's commitment to accurately recounting the
past. According to Brettler, not every ancient account of the past

---

[22]   Genesis 5:28-29.

is written in the same way and for the same purposes. Some are more committed to accurately recounting the past than others. Some are more interested in entertaining the reader than others.[23] But in all cases, the writer's distinctive ideology and/or theology will guide how he or she recounts the past.[24]

Take, for instance, 1-2 Chronicles (hereafter just "Chronicles"). Chronicles is a rewriting of earlier biblical texts, especially 1-2 Samuel and 1-2 Kings (hereafter just "Samuel" and "Kings"). Yet, it is evident that the Chronicler introduces into his version of many biblical stories a number of changes that conflict with the corresponding passages in Samuel and Kings. Julius Wellhausen, the famed nineteenth-century biblical scholar, contends that the differences in the Chronicler's history rest not on early sources but on contemporary "prevailing ideas."[25] Ultimately, he concludes that much of the Chronicler's work is ideological, propagandist fiction masked in a mere historical facade:

---

[23]   See, for example, the impulsive and absurd measures taken by King Ahasuerus that are recorded in the first chapter of Esther. Those who produced the Aramaic version of Esther (Targum Rishon and Targum Sheni – see chapter 8) depict Ahasuerus in an even worse light by having him order Queen Vashti to appear before him and his court naked with only a crown on her head:

> He responded and said to them, "Go and say to Queen Vashti, 'Arise from your royal throne, strip naked, and place the golden crown on your head, a golden cup in your right hand, and a golden jug in your left hand, and enter before me and before the 127 kings who wear the crown in order that they may see you, that you are more beautiful than all women.'" (Dost, "Esther 1")

[24]   Brettler, *The Creation of Israel*, 1. Similarly, Sternberg, *The Poetics of Biblical Narrative: Ideological Literature and the Drama of Reading*, 44.
[25]   Wellhausen, *Prolegomena to the History of Ancient Israel*, 172.

See what Chronicles has made out of David! The founder of the kingdom has become the founder of the Temple and the public worship, the king and hero at the head of his companions in arms has become the singer and master of ceremonies at the head of a swarm of priests and Levites; his clearly cut figure has become a feeble holy picture, seen through a cloud of incense. It is obviously vain to try to combine the fundamentally different portraits into one stereoscopic image; it is only the tradition of the older source that possesses historical value.[26]

Furthermore, he asserts that the liberties taken by the writer of Chronicles are done in part to make Israel's past look more Jewish, which in his view is sheer deception.[27]

While most scholars now consider many of Wellhausen's views to be out of fashion or simply inaccurate, some of his nineteenth-century views have been revived by the "minimalist" or "revisionist" camp of latter twentieth-century scholarship, of which P. R. Davies is representative. In the well-known work *In Search of "Ancient Israel,"* for instance, Davies, like other minimalists, reads biblical historiography through the postmodern lenses of suspicion and skepticism, which produces a reading of the biblical text that is far more radical than Wellhausen's. He considers objectivity as a delusion and argues that history, like memories, involves the ordering, selecting, interpreting, and distorting of events by the historiographer, which means that historiography is fiction.[28]

Davies is indeed correct in declaring that (hi)stories have an end in mind; the reasoning that leads him to the conclusion that biblical narrative is fiction is not sound, however. He asserts, first, that if historiography is literature, and literature is ideology, then all historiography must be ideology. Taking it further, he asserts that if all historiography is ideology, and

---

[26]   Ibid., 182.
[27]   Ibid., 223.
[28]   Davies, *In Search of "Ancient Israel:" A Study in Biblical Origins*, 13.

ideology is fiction, then all historiography is fiction. Both syllogisms are logically flawed, and this brand of scholarship is not representative of the mainstream.

Wheaton College professor of Old Testament John Walton provides a more sober perspective. He observes that ancient Near Eastern historiography (and this includes ancient Israelite historiography) differs from post-Enlightenment historiography—that to which we are most accustomed—in that it often asks different questions, goes about answering questions differently, and is driven by worldviews that are in many ways very different from our own.[29] The writers of the Hebrew Bible are often presenting Israel and Judah's past from a perspective of faith, which is why Fleming may rightly quip, "The Bible would make a fascinating historical source, if only we could figure out how to use it as such."[30]

***

What does all of the foregoing have to do with our investigation into when, where, and by whom the Bible was written? In short, everything. In order to answer these questions, we must first settle the questions of to what degree and in which ways biblical historiography corresponds with the reality on the ground in ancient Israel. Our perspective on the historical reliability of the Exodus traditions will shape our understanding of the level of involvement that Moses could have had in writing the Hebrew Bible's first five books. Our assessment of the trustworthiness of the Hebrew Bible's accounts of David and Solomon will impact our decisions about David's and Solomon's contributions to the biblical books that are traditionally ascribed to them.

---

[29]   Walton, *Ancient Near Eastern Thought and the Old Testament*, 189-211.

[30]   Fleming, *The Legacy of Judah's Bible: History, Politics, and the Reinscribing of the Tradition*, 3.

Furthermore, an awareness of Israelite and Judean history allows one to more confidently determine what a given texts can and cannot mean. One example is the "Immanuel" prophecy of Isaiah 7. According to the Gospel of Matthew, Jesus' birth by the virgin Mary took place to "fulfil" Isaiah's prophecy:

> *Now all of this happened in order to fulfil what was spoken by the Lord through the prophets: "Behold, the virgin will conceive and will bear a son, and they will call his name 'Immanuel,'" which is translated, "God is with us."* (Matthew 1:22-23)

What Matthew means by "fulfil" is a matter that we will address in the next chapter. For now, though, it is important to recognize, first of all, that the text that Matthew presents is not a Greek translation of the Masoretic text. Instead, it is the Greek text of Isaiah that was produced sometime around the mid-second century BCE.[31] And as we will see in chapter 8, the Greek Old Testament, commonly called the Septuagint, is not a literal translation of the Masoretic Text. While the Greek version of Isaiah predicts that a virgin *will conceive* sometime in the future, the Masoretic text says that a young woman of marriageable age—not a virgin—*has already conceived* at the time the prophecy occurred, sometime around 732 BCE. This means that Isaiah was not speaking about Jesus of Nazareth, who would be born approximately eight hundred years later. The text makes it clear, in fact, that by the time the child "knows good and evil," Aram (i.e., Syria) and the Northern Kingdom Israel would no longer be (Isaiah 7:8, 16). Furthermore, the Immanuel child was promised to be a sign to the eighth-century king Ahaz. Were the Immanuel child Jesus, God's sign would be of no use to Ahaz, who was long since dead at the time of Jesus' birth. Thus, awareness of Israelite and Judean historical context is important

---

[31] Hengel, *The Septuagint as Christian Scripture: Its Prehistory and the Problem of Its Canon*, 85.

for the history of biblical interpretation as well as for understanding the context in which the Hebrew Bible was written.

I consider the material covered in this chapter to be of critical importance for fostering Bible-centered dialogue. Many readers of the Hebrew Bible are interested in what biblical scholars have to say, but they have not yet learned how scholarly arguments are developed or how a standard scholarly approach to Israelite and Judean history may contrast with a "literal"[32] reading of the text. While the foregoing may run contrary to what one may hear in church on a Sunday morning or at a Wednesday night Bible study, it is important for all readers of the Bible who are interested in engaging in faith-related dialogue with those outside of their own circles to understand these distinctives (regardless of whether or not they agree!). After all, these are the perspectives that are taught in many university Bible and theology courses, and these are the perspectives that underpin the perspectives presented by many scholars featured in Bible-related documentaries and media productions.[33]

---

[32] I should note here that I try at all cost to avoid the term "literal," as I have found it to be incorrectly understood by many to indicate an approach to reading that is free of interpretation. Because no approach to reading any text is free of interpretation, I prefer the term "contextual," as it takes seriously the historical, linguistic, and literary contexts of a given passage. For further discussion and relevant bibliography, see Garfinkel, "Applied *Peshat*: Historical-Critical Method and Religious Meaning," 19-28.

[33] One such example is "The Bible Unearthed." http://www.salem-news.com/articles/january282012/bible-unearthed-ae.php.

4
THE HEBREW BIBLE AS LITERATURE

The twenty-seven documents that comprise the New Testament were composed in Greek.[1] The Greek of the New Testament, however, is very different from the Classical Greek of Homer, Plato, and Aristotle, and the striking difference between these two forms of Greek gave rise in the nineteenth century to the idea that the New Testament was written in a divinely inspired language, which some called "Holy Ghost Greek."[2] This hypothesis was short-lived, however, for in the late nineteenth century it was discovered that this form of Greek, now known as Koine Greek, was used widely in antiquity.[3]

---

[1] There are some who argue that certain documents of the New Testament were written in Hebrew or Aramaic. Until recently, the general consensus has been that Jesus' mother tongue was Aramaic and not Hebrew, and indeed, there is substantial evidence to support this view (e.g., Fitzmyer, *The Semitic Background of the New Testament*, 2.6-10. For a discussion of evidence supporting Aramaic Q sources, see Casey, *An Aramaic Approach to Q: Sources for the Gospels of Matthew and Luke*, 185-90). Interestingly, for all his emphasis on the Aramaic background of the New Testament, Black supposes that Jesus was as comfortable in Hebrew as he was in Aramaic (*An Aramaic Approach to the Gospels and the Acts* [3rd ed.], 49), though he does see heavy Aramaic influence in the sayings of Jesus (ibid., 271-74.) The fourth-century CE *Ecclesiastical History* of Eusebius records that the second-century CE Papias of Hierapolis claimed, "Matthew compiled the oracles in the Hebrew language; but everyone interpreted them as he was able" (Eusebius, *Ecclesiastical History*, 3.39.16). Moreover, recent scholarship has presented an abundance of evidence that support not only the notion that Hebrew was spoken in Palestine in Jesus' day (Schniedewind, *A Social History of Hebrew: Its Origins Through the Rabbinic Period*, 164-92), but that it was actually Jesus' mother tongue (see Buth and Notley, eds., *The Language Environment of First Century Judaea*).

[2] Porter, "Language and Translation of the New Testament," 185-86.

[3] For a brief overview of the Greek language and some of the distinctives of Koine Greek and New Testament Greek, see Wallace, 14-30.

Similarly, in Jesus' day, Hebrew was also thought to have been the language of heaven, unlike Aramaic or Greek.[4] Nevertheless, there can be no doubt that the Hebrew of the Scriptures is very much a human language that descended not from heaven but from other Semitic languages.[5] In 1868, a victory monument—also known as a "stela"—dating to the ninth-century BCE, the time of the Israelite kings Omri and Ahab, was discovered in what today is the country of Jordan. During the time of Omri and Ahab, however, this was the land of the Moabites, a people group that figures significantly in ancient Israel's history and who were, we are told in Ruth 4:17-22, ancestors of King David. This victory monument—the Mesha Stela—describes a conflict between Moab and Israel that is also recorded in 2 Kings 3. The inscription is not only written in roughly the same script used in Israel during the monarchical period, but it is written in a language that bears such striking resemblance to Hebrew that there can be no doubt that biblical Hebrew, just like biblical Greek, is not in any way a divine or "Holy Ghost" language.[6]

It is not just the script and the language in which it is written that show the Hebrew Bible to be a product of its time and environment. Countless passages and even entire books are influenced by and sometimes modeled on ancient Near Eastern

---

For a more detailed history of Koine Greek, see Adrados, *A History of the Greek Language from Its Origins to the Present*, 175-225.

[4]   Jubilees 12:26-27. This notion is also perpetuated in rabbinic sources, as well (e.g., b. Sotah 33a; Genesis Rabbah 1.4, 10; 52.5).

[5]   The Semitic language family includes a number of languages from the ancient Near East, all of which are in some way akin to Hebrew. The best-known examples are Akkadian, Aramaic, and Arabic. For a brief survey of the interrelationship of the Semitic languages, see Rubin, *A Brief Introduction to the Semitic Languages*, 3-6. For a discussion of the relationship of Moabite and Hebrew, see Aḥituv's presentation and discussion of the Mesha Stela (Aḥituv, *Echoes from the Past: Hebrew and Cognate Inscriptions from the Biblical Period*, 389-418).

[6]   Similarly, the Aramaic portions of the Hebrew Bible are written in an attested dialect known as "Imperial Aramaic," which was used throughout the Assyrian, Babylonian, and Persian empires.

literary forms and genres. In certain cases, in fact, scholars are able to convincingly demonstrate that the writers of certain biblical works drew heavily from specific ancient Near Eastern texts that are now known to us. The numerous parallels between the Hebrew Bible and ancient Near Eastern literature has given rise to what is often called "the comparative approach" to biblical interpretation.[7] To illustrate the importance of genre analysis and the comparative approach to the Hebrew Bible, we will examine Genesis' first creation account (1:1-2:4a) and selections from the book of Isaiah.

The First Creation Account

Genesis 1 is commonly understood as a straightforward account of how God created the cosmos, and in modern times this text is regularly used by conservatives as the foundation for polemics against evolution and homosexual lifestyles, as the passage identifies God as the creator of human life and the institution of heterosexual marriage (Genesis 1:26-31). What most readers miss, however, is that the intended meaning of an ancient Near Eastern creation account is not to be found on the surface of the waters, as it were.

To discover why a text was written, it is often helpful to carefully examine the author's choices of words and themes. A

---

[7]   For a detailed treatment of the comparative approach, see Walton, *Ancient Near Eastern Thought and the Old Testament: Introducing the Conceptual World of the Hebrew Bible* (2nd ed.), 3-44. This work is particularly useful because it (1) explains the comparative approach and its place in the field of scholarship, (2) surveys the relevant ancient Near Eastern literature, and (3) explores how some of the more important concepts pertaining to Israel's history, society, and religion are informed by recourse to ancient Near Eastern parallel literature.

The classic anthology of comparative literature is Pritchard's *Ancient Near Eastern Texts Relating to the Old Testament*. A much more user-friendly and up-to-date anthology is Hallo and Younger, Jr., *The Context of Scripture* (hereafter, "*COS*"), which contains extensive footnotes and references to the Hebrew Scriptures.

careful examination of Genesis 1:1-2:4a[8] reveals that some of the passage's key terms are very much at home in the priestly book of Leviticus. Five times in Genesis 1 we read of God creating by "separating" one thing from another (Genesis 1:4, 6, 7, 14, 18). This is the same term that is used in Leviticus 10:10, where God commands Israel to distinguish that which is sacred and clean from that which is profane and unclean. The importance that separation and division play in Leviticus can be seen in 20:24-26:

> *I have said to you, "You will inherit the land that I will give you to possess, a land flowing with milk and honey. I am the* LORD *your God, who separated you from among the gentiles. You must separate the clean beast from the unclean, and the unclean bird from the clean. You must not contaminate yourselves with beast, with bird, or with anything that crawls on the ground, which I have distinguished as unclean with respect to you. Be sanctified with respect to me, for I, the* LORD, *am sanctified, and I have distinguished you from the nations to be mine.*

Additionally, God concludes the week of creation by resting on the Sabbath, a concept that pervades the latter chapters of Leviticus. Furthermore, the creation of the celestial luminaries to mark "signs, appointed times, days, and years" (Genesis 1:14) likely reflects the priestly interest in the religious calendar (see, e.g., Leviticus 23-23). These and other considerations have led scholars to regard the Bible's first creation account as a "priestly" account of creation.[9] But before we discuss the significance of these findings, we must also look at the Bible's first creation account in the light of another ancient Near Eastern creation account.

---

[8]   The division between chapters 1 and 2 should have been placed after the first half of the second chapter's fourth verse (Genesis 2:4a).

[9]   E.g., Walton, *Ancient Near Eastern Thought and the Old Testament*, 146-47; M. S. Smith, *The Priestly Vision of Genesis 1*, 87-114.

Both the content and the function of the Bible's first creation account resemble the content and function of other Near Eastern creation accounts. However, the one that has received the most attention is the Babylonian "Epic of Creation," which is often referred to by its first two words, *Enuma Elish*.[10]

Enuma Elish (EE) was composed in the late second millennium BCE,[11] long before the time when many scholars think that Genesis 1:1-2:4a was written. The story begins at a time when the gods were not yet created. According to the text, all that existed at that time were the female Tiamat and the male Apsu, from whom the gods were created. Apsu is the personification of the fresh water, and Tiamat is the personification of the salty, ocean water, and the gods were created by the "mingling of their waters" (EE 1.5). This is similar to the beginning of Genesis 1, which tells us that before God began to create, there already existed a water world:

> *When God began to create the heavens and the earth, the earth was without form and void and darkness was upon the face of the deep, while the spirit of God hovered over the face of the waters.*

The Hebrew word translated as "deep" in Genesis 1:2 is *tehom*, which is etymologically related to the Akkadian name "Tiamat." Furthermore, in *Enuma Elish*, once the god Marduk defeats Tiamat in battle, he splits her carcass (effectively "separating the waters from the waters") and from it establishes the heavens (EE 6.123-40). It is impossible to miss the connection with Genesis 1:6-8:

> *And God said, "Let there be an expanse in the midst of the water, and let it separate the water."*[12] *So God made the*

---

[10]   Foster, *Before the Muses: An Anthology of Akkadian Literature*, 436-86, for a translation of the text and important bibliography.

[11]   Ibid., 486.

[12]   Literally, "let it separate between water and water."

expanse, and he separated the water that was beneath the expanse and the water that was above the expanse. And it was so. And God called the expanse "sky." And there was evening, and there was morning: a second day.

The splitting of Tiamat's carcass is followed soon after by the marking of time (EE 5.1ff.), which resembles Genesis 1:14-16, where it is said that God creates the sun, moon, and stars to establish seasons, as we observed above.

As interesting as this may be, we must ask, How does this information help us to better understand the process of the Hebrew Bible's formation? To answer this question in a convincing way, we must explain how the priestly elements of the creation account and the Babylonian parallels are interrelated. When in the course of their history would Israelites and/or Judeans have been preoccupied with both priestly matters and with Babylonian culture, and why? If we are to assume, as many conservative historians do, that Moses wrote this story sometime around the mid-thirteenth century BCE, then the Babylonians would have been of no concern. After all, why would the Israelites have been concerned with matters pertaining to Babylonia at a time when they were spinning their wheels in the wilderness bordering Egypt, far from the seat of southern Mesopotamian power? And besides, Babylon had enough problems of its own at that time to have been interested in the inconsequential, desert-dwelling Israelites.[13] The powerful Kassite dynasty of Babylonia was under threat in the mid-thirteenth century BCE and eventually conquered by the Assyrian emperor Tukulti-Ninurta in 1225 BCE, the very time when many conservatives would have Moses writing the Torah.

---

[13]   Van De Mieroop, *A History of the Ancient Near East ca. 3000-323 BC*, 170-89; Kuhrt, *The Ancient Near East c. 3000-330 BC*, 332-81. It is worth noting, however, that Mesopotamian literature was well known and influential throughout the Near East during this period (Van De Mieroop, 178-79). Most, I think, would find it highly unlikely that the Israelite refugees would have had access to this literature, however.

In fact, the Babylonians were of no concern until the end of the seventh century, when Assyrian power was rapidly waning. It is during this time, the time of the prophet Jeremiah and his younger contemporary Ezekiel, that both Babylon and the idea of Torah observance were of great concern to ancient Israel.[14] Ezekiel, who was both a prophet and a priest (Ezekiel 1:3), was exiled to Babylon in the early sixth century BCE, approximately one decade before the Babylonians destroyed Yahweh's temple, razed Jerusalem, and exiled much of the Judean population. It was during this time that the people of the LORD had to wrestle with questions of ethnic, cultural, and religious identity, for, we are told, it was the will of God that they should not soon return from Babylon. And for this reason, Jeremiah was told to instruct them:

> *Build houses, and settle. Plant gardens, and eat their produce.*
> *Take wives, and produce sons and daughters. Take wives for*
> *your sons, and give your daughters to men so that they may*
> *produce sons and daughters. Multiply there, and do not*
> *remain small.*[15]

While they were to take spouses, they were not to take foreigners (i.e., Babylonians) for spouses. From a biblical perspective, marriage to non-Israelites led to the corruption of worship (1 Kings 11:1-13), which was considered to be a violation of Israel's treaty with God (Deuteronomy 5:1-8; 17:14-17). The will of God was that his people remain distinct (2 Kings 17:15).

In order to remind the exiles to remain faithful to their covenant with God and to refrain from assimilating into Babylonian culture and religion, the writers of Genesis 1:1-2:4a do what certain Mesopotamian texts do: they project back to the beginning of time the idea or behavior that they endorse.[16] So it is possible that the creation account of Genesis 1:1-2:4a was

---

[14]   Cf. M. S. Smith, *The Priestly Vision of Genesis 1*, 41-43.

[15]   Jeremiah 29:5-6.

[16]   E.g., Glassner, *Mesopotamian Chronicles*, 117-26.

written as it was in order to exhort those familiar with the annual recitation of *Enuma Elish* during the Babylonian New Year's festival[17] to be imitators of their God and maintain their distinct identity by keeping Sabbath (and presumably other religious obligations).

Without carefully examining the genre of the first creation account and reading it in the light of other biblical and ancient Near Eastern literature, we would incorrectly date the work and misread its message, both of which would affect our understanding of the overall development of the Hebrew Bible.[18]

Prophetic Texts

One of the hallmarks of biblical prophecy is the expression "Thus saith the LORD."[19] It occurs roughly three hundred times, in all three sections of the Hebrew Bible. This expression is not unique to Israelite and Judean prophecy, however. Approximately one millennium before Israel's and Judah's first writing prophets—Hosea, Amos, Isaiah, and Micah— Mesopotamian prophecies were recorded in writing in the Amorite city of Mari on the upper Euphrates river, in what today is Tell Ḥarīrī, Syria.[20] Included among the over 20,000 clay tablets to have been discovered there are records of prophesies, which bear a number of formal correspondences with Israelite prophesy. Many of the letters use expressions similar to "Thus saith the LORD." One such example is found in a letter from Nur-

---

[17] Van De Mieroop, *A History of the Ancient Near East*, 178.

[18] The reader may find instructive Walton's comments on the problems of reading Genesis 1 as a science textbook (Walton, *The Lost World of Genesis One: Ancient Cosmology and the Origins Debate*, 162-63).

[19] A more accurate translation of this expression is "This is what Yahweh (= "the LORD") says."

[20] One may view the site by simply conducting a search for "Tell Hariri, Syria" via https://www.google.com/earth/.

Sin to Zimri-Lim in which the prophet Abiya is said to have begun his prophecy with "Thus says (the god) Adad."[21]

The correspondence between Mari and Israelite prophecy goes far beyond this shared formula, though. Within just this letter we encounter numerous other similarities. For one, we learn that prophets are not necessarily responsible for the writing of their own prophecies. Such is the case in the aforementioned letter. Abiya's prophecy is recorded in a letter from Nur-Sin to Zimri-Lim. And while within the Hebrew Bible we can find references to prophets writing (e.g., Isaiah 8:1; Ezekiel 24:2), certain biblical texts give us an indication that Israelite and Judean prophets sometimes had their prophecies written down by someone else. In the book of Jeremiah, for instance, we are told that his scribe Baruch is responsible for the written record of his oracles (e.g., Jeremiah 36:4, 17-18; 36:32), and one can only assume that he contributed to the oracles' framework in some way.

We also see in some of these prophetic texts from Mari examples of multiple prophetic texts having been added to the same clay tablet. This supports what biblical scholars have long suspected, that scrolls containing ancient Israelite prophecies were supplemented and expanded, sometimes centuries after the original scroll was composed. For example, the numerous references to Zion and Jerusalem in Amos are evidently not from Amos himself, as his prophetic activity concerned Israel, not Judah and its capital Jerusalem (Amos 1:1). These were added at a later date, sometime after the end of the Northern Kingdom in the late eighth century BCE. Similarly, the references to Babylon in the book of Isaiah (e.g., Isaiah 13:1) must come from a later author since Babylon would have been of no consequence to an eighth century BCE Judean prophet.

---

[21] For the text and a translation of the letter, see Níssínen, *Prophets and Prophecy in the Ancient Near East*, 21-22. For a broad overview of ancient Near Eastern prophecy, see Níssínen, *Prophecy in Its Ancient Near Eastern Context: Mesopotamian, Biblical, and Arabian Perspectives*.

There is no doubt that Israelite and Judean prophecy has its own distinguishing features.[22] However, the similarities with Mesopotamian prophetic texts are so striking that we cannot disregard them. On the basis of the significant correspondences between the prophetic texts from Israel and Mari, we may conclude that:

1. Israelite and Judean prophecies were not necessarily recorded by the individual after whom the book is named. Amos did not necessarily record the contents of the document that we call "The Book of Amos." Isaiah did not necessarily record the contents of the document that we call "The Book of Isaiah." While some avid Bible readers may find this shocking, such a conclusion should not be considered unorthodox, since many of the prophecies of the Hebrew Bible are introduced in the third person by an anonymous voice. Furthermore, since Bible readers are fully aware that Jesus did not compose the gospels, we should not be surprised to discover that many of the Hebrew Bible's "writing" prophets did not compose the texts attributed to them.

2. We should not assume that any of the Hebrew Bible's prophetic books are the work of one author. In fact, given what we have learned about the expansion of texts in the ancient world and in non-prophetic biblical books, our operating assumption should be that every biblical book is the work of more than one author over the course of many centuries.

---

[22] For a comprehensive introduction to Israelite and Judean prophecy, see Joseph Blenkinsopp, *A History of Prophecy in Israel.*

Conclusion

We have established in our discussion of Genesis and Isaiah just how important genre analysis and the comparative approach are for understanding the Hebrew Bible and its development. Were it not for space constraints, we could explore the influence of Sargon of Akkad's birth legend upon the story of Moses' birth,[23] or the dependence of the Covenant Code (Exodus 20:22-23:33) upon the Code of Hammurabi,[24] or the resemblance of the conquest narrative in Joshua 9-12 to Egyptian military texts.[25] We could show the influence of Zoroastrianism's apocalypses upon the book of Daniel,[26] or the relationship of Psalm 29 to an earlier Phoenician hymn.[27] We could address the dependence of Proverbs 22:17-23:14 upon the Egyptian Instructions of Amenemope,[28] or fill pages discussing the heavy dependence of the story of Noah's Ark upon the Akkadian Epic of Gilgamesh.[29]

Wherever one stands theologically, it is clear, as 2 Peter 2:20-21 indicates, that human beings were the ones who wrote and copied the Hebrew Scriptures. And unless we approach the individual texts of the Hebrew Scriptures on their own terms, we cannot get to the bottom of when and by whom they were written. We continue our discussion in the next chapter by examining literacy rates and the process of text production in ancient Israel so that we may better understand who was (and was not) capable of producing biblical texts and what it would take for them to accomplish such a task.

---

[23]   *COS* 1.133.

[24]   *COS* 2.131.

[25]   Lawson Younger, Jr., *Ancient Conquest Accounts: A Study in Ancient Near Eastern and Biblical History Writing*, 265.

[26]   Mary Boyce, *Textual Studies for the Study of Zoroastrianism*, 90-96.

[27]   Gaster, "Psalm 29."

[28]   *COS* 1.47.

[29]   *ANET* 72-99. For a comprehensive overview of texts from the ancient world that have parallels in the Hebrew Bible, see Sparks, *Ancient Texts for the Study of the Hebrew Bible*.

5
LITERACY & TEXT PRODUCTION

One of the mistakes we tend to make in studying ancient texts is that we read them against the backdrop of our own modern Western culture. Too often, we assume that the social norms of our world were the norms of the biblical world. We incorrectly assume that the social roles (such as father, mother, priest, and king) and the social institutions (such as marriage, divorce, adoption, and slavery) of ancient Israel that we encounter in the Hebrew Bible are closely akin to their modern Western counterparts. This is never more true as when we read biblical texts that mention authorship and book production. As we will see, when it comes to education, literacy, and the production of literature, ancient Israel and twenty-first century America could hardly be more distinct from one another.

Take, for instance, the concept of the "book." In the twenty-first century West, a book is a composition, generally written by one or two authors, which is printed on leaves of paper, which are then stacked, bound, and covered. Once a book is published the work is finished for good, unless the author wants to update it. In such cases, the revised version is given a new ISBN ("International Standard Book Number") and is ultimately considered a new book. And as any college student ought to know, if an author chooses to include in her own work portions of another author's work, the dictates of Western culture demand that she acknowledge as much in an in-text citation or a footnote. A student who plagiarizes may receive a failing grade for his assignment or, for repeated offences, be expelled from school. A professional who plagiarizes may lose his job or be sued. Ancient Near Eastern writers,[1] however, operated according to very different standards, which impacted

---

[1]   I intentionally avoid the term "author" here because of the connotations that the term bears for a modern Western audience.

ancient Israelite scribal culture and ultimately the development of the Hebrew Bible.[2]

Then there is the matter of literacy and education. For many today, literacy is something that is taken for granted. It is generally expected that parents will send their children to school by around the age of five in order to begin developing, among other skills, the ability to read and write. Because illiteracy is generally viewed today as the exception rather than the rule, many make the mistake of assuming that such was the case in ancient Israel. This, however, is an unwarranted assumption, and one that significantly impacts our perceptions about who was and was not able to create the literature of the Hebrew Bible. And it is with this matter that we begin our investigation into the scribal culture of ancient Israel.

Literacy

According to the National Assessment of Adult Literacy, as of 2003 the percentage of the United States population "lacking basic prose literary skills" was as low as six percent in Minnesota, New Hampshire, and North Dakota but as high as twenty-three percent in California, with New York coming in a close second at twenty-two percent.[3] While to many, New York's and California's relatively low literacy rates are unfathomable in this day and age, they are extraordinarily high when compared with literacy rates in the ancient Near East.[4] In the ancient world, few learned how to read and write because their agrarian lifestyle did not afford them the opportunity to

---

[2]   Note, however, the importance that Jewish tradition places upon the citing of sources (Weinberg, "Citation, Obliteration, and Plagiarism, as Discussed in Ancient Jewish Sources," 2337-64).

[3]   https://nces.ed.gov/naal/estimates/StateEstimates.aspx.   Accessed 8/1/ 2018.

[4]   For a discussion of language and literacy in the ancient Near East, see Bard, *An Introduction the Archaeology of Ancient Egypt*, 27-34; Radner and Robson, eds., *The Oxford Handbook of Cuneiform Culture*, 5-112.

attain literacy,[5] and the harsh climate of Middle Eastern deserts only exacerbated matters.[6] Furthermore, even if a sedentary or nomadic farmer could read or write, he would have had little opportunity to materially benefit from possessing such a skill set.

Some may be surprised at this, particularly since writing dates back to as early as the latter half of the fourth millennium BCE. Sumerian, the predominant language of Mesopotamia until ca. 2000 BCE, is attested from the southern Mesopotamian city of Uruk/Warka (biblical Erech [Genesis 10:10]) from approximately 3200 BCE.[7] Egyptian writing is almost as old, appearing within the next two centuries,[8] perhaps as a result of Uruk's broad influence.[9]

Before we can determine what percentage of an ancient people group is literate, we need to determine what we mean by literacy. Are we talking about professional competency or merely the ability to write at a rudimentary level? Baines, who is interested in the "professionally literate," estimates that in Old Kingdom Egypt no more than one percent of the population was literate.[10] However, he recognizes that there are exceptions to the rule. For instance, in the New Kingdom community of Deir

---

[5] We should note, however, that the cuneiform (wedge-shaped) script used in Mesopotamia for the Sumerian and Akkadian languages developed from "ideographic tablets," which recorded transactions (Englund, "Accounting in Proto-Cuneiform," 34).

[6] MacDonald, "Literacy in an Oral Environment," 51.

[7] For a concise discussion of the earliest period of Mesopotamian literacy, see Roaf, *Cultural Atlas of Mesopotamia and the Ancient Near East*, 56-63, 70. For more detailed treatment, see Nissen, *The Early History of the Ancient Near East: 9000-2000 B.C.*, 65-127. For an extensive discussion of the sociohistorical context in which Mesopotamian writing developed, see Algaze, *The Uruk World System: The Dynamics of Expansion of Early Mesopotamian Civilization* (2d ed.).

[8] Rubio, "The Languages of the Ancient Near East," 85.

[9] Van De Mieroop, *A History of Ancient Egypt*, 47-48. For early evidence of trade between Egypt and Mesopotamia, see Mark, *From Egypt to Mesopotamia: A Study in Predynastic Trade Routes*.

[10] Baines, *Visual and Written Culture in Ancient Egypt*, 67.

el Medina, literacy seems to have been between 5.0-7.5%.[11] But as Baines notes, defining what does and does not constitute literacy is a sticky issue.[12] Determining the prevalence of literacy in ancient Mesopotamia and Greece is fraught with similar problems.[13]

In his overview of literacy in the ancient Eastern Mediterranean world, Van Der Toorn proposes the following rates of literacy: Greece – 10%; Egypt – 7%; Mesopotamia – 5%.[14] Even if these figures are too high, they demonstrate that in the Eastern Mediterranean world to which ancient Israel belonged, literate persons were the exception rather than the rule.[15] This is true even in societies in which alphabetic scripts were used, including ancient Israel.[16]

Van Der Toorn does not hazard a guess as to the rate of literacy in ancient Israel, but he, like Carr, observes that ancient Israel was a predominantly oral society,[17] which suggests that ancient Israel's rate of literacy would have been very low. Some of the Hebrew inscriptions from Israel's and Judah's respective monarchical periods could be interpreted as evidence in favor of a higher literacy rate. One such example is found in a collection of inscriptions discovered at Lachish, the second-most fortified

---

[11]   Ibid., 94.

[12]   Ibid., 33-35, 89-92. Likewise, Veldhuis, "Levels of Literacy."

[13]   See, for example, Foster & Foster's discussion of the early second millennium BCE Assyrian colony outside of Kanesh (*Civilizations of Ancient Iraq*, 106).

[14]   Van Der Toorn, *Scribal Culture and the Making of the Hebrew Bible*, 10.

[15]   In fact, not all Mesopotamian and Egyptian kings claim to be able to read. In Mesopotamia, such claims are rare (ibid., 63). Nevertheless, there were many kings who were literate, and in earlier Mesopotamian history, many kings may have arisen from the scribal community (Frahm, "Keeping Company with Men of Learning: The King as Scholar," 508-32).

[16]   Rollston, "The Phoenician Script of the Tel Zayit Abecedary and Putative Evidence for Israelite Literacy," 57-70; Van Der Toorn, *Scribal Culture*, 11.

[17]   Van Der Toorn, *Scribal Culture*, 10; Carr, *Writing on the Tablets of the Heart*, 13.

Judean site, located approximately twenty-five miles south-west of Jerusalem. The inscriptions are presumably drafts of letters written during 588 or 587 (shortly before the destruction of the city by King Nebuchadnezzar II of Babylon (see Jeremiah 34:6-7) from Lachish by one military official, Hoshayahu, to another, Yaush, who was located in Jerusalem.[18] In the third letter, Hoshayahu affirms to Yaush in the strongest terms that he is capable of reading letters containing military correspondence.[19] While the written exchange between the two individuals, who presumably did not belong to Judean society's upper crust, could be taken as evidence of an increase in literacy, the contents of the letter may indicate that even at the end of the Judean monarchy, literacy among military officials was by no means a given.

The earliest inscriptions that have been presented as evidence for literacy in ancient Israel are the Tel Zayit Abecedary and the Gezer Calendar, both of which date to the tenth century BCE. The Tel Zayit Abecedary is an alphabetic inscription (hence the classification "abecedary"), which was written on a stone that came to be incorporated into a tenth-century wall at the site of Tel Zayit, which is located approximately twenty-four miles to the south-west of Jerusalem. Unfortunately, we cannot be sure if the inscription is Israelite because the site is located in an area that regularly changed hands between the Israelites and the Philistines.[20]

As for the Gezer Calendar, Aḥituv suggests that it should be dated between ca. 950 – ca. 925 BCE; and since Gezer was under Solomonic control at that time, the inscription should be considered Israelite. And even if one does not consider the text to be Israelite,[21] its very presence in an area that came to be controlled by Solomon coupled with the numerous inscriptions

[18]   Lindenberger, *Ancient Aramaic and Hebrew Letters*, 102-3.
[19]   Ibid., 111-12.
[20]   Tappy, "Tel Zayit and the Tel Zayit Abededary in Their Regional Context," 37.
[21]   Carr, "The Tel Zayit Abecedary in (Social) Context," 119.

found in the Levant during Israel's early days suggests that literacy was attested at least in the highest strata of Israelite culture at that time.[22] This supports the more conservative conclusion that portions of the Bible could have been written in the earliest centuries of Israel's monarchical period.

Text Production

Ancient Israel has left behind relatively little direct evidence concerning text production, but fortunately, its Mesopotamian and Egyptian neighbors did. While we cannot comprehensively explore this subject here, I would like to present a few characteristics of ancient Near Eastern text production that may help us to draw reasonable inferences of how texts were created in ancient Israel.[23]

First, for whatever their scribal and literary achievements, oral transmission of texts was far more common in the cultures of the ancient Near East.[24] From Sumerian evidence we learn that many texts were written from memory and were not intended to be preserved.[25] This is evident from the practice of "tablet refurbishing"[26] in eighteenth century BCE Nibru.[27] This may explain some (though certainly not all) of the discrepancies between parallel accounts in the Hebrew Bible, such as those found in Chronicles and Kings.[28] Discrepancies in parallel biblical texts may result from copying errors, but may

---

[22]   Of particular interest is the Khirbet Qeiyafa ostraca, which appears to be early evidence of state formation. See Millard, "The Ostracon from the Days of David found at Khirbet Qeiyafa."

[23]   For a detailed treatment of this subject, see Carr, *Writing on the Tablets of the Heart.*

[24]   Ibid., 81-82.

[25]   Black et al., *The Literature of Ancient Sumer*, 275.

[26]   Ibid., xlii.

[27]   Ibid., 275.

[28]   Person Jr., *The Deuteronomic History and the Book of Chronicles: Scribal Works in an Oral World*, 43-51, especially 47.

also result from misremembering and mishearing orally circulated and orally transmitted "texts."[29]

Second, and related to the foregoing, scribes memorized large portions of the literary "classics," and this would surely have been the case in ancient Israelite scribal training.[30] And if we are to take our cue from what we have learned from Sumerian scribal culture, then it stands to reason that Israelite and Judean scribes would have copied and even memorized large portions of text from a wide variety of genres. The oral transmission and memorization of texts were also an integral part of rabbinic culture. Texts often held a more ceremonial function, and the practice of "reading for information" could be considered heretical and perilous.[31] What a striking contrast with Protestant tradition and the Islamic characterization of Jews (and Christians) as *ahl al-kitaab* ("The People of the Book").[32] Now there is no denying that Hittite, Mesopotamian, Egyptian, and Persian texts directly influenced biblical authors and that some of these texts were used for scribal training. After all, many scribes were in the employ of the state for both religious and non-religious purposes and would have needed to have been trained with as much breadth as depth. This would help to explain why there are so many parallels between biblical texts and earlier Near Eastern texts. We must conclude, however, that the copying of these ancient texts was done from memory some of the time, which means that the same is probably true for the "copying" of biblical texts.

Third, in many cases, authorship and dating of ancient texts are difficult to determine, in part, because anonymity was the order of the day. There are exceptions, but in the main,

---

[29]   Black et al., *The Literature of Ancient Sumer*, xlviii.
[30]   Van Der Toorn, *Scribal Culture*, 56.
[31]   Wollenberg, "The Dangers of Reading as We Know It: Sight Reading As a Source of Heresy in Early Rabbinic Traditions," 711-12, 728. I thank Robert Harris for sharing these insights and directing me to this resource.
[32]   E.g., Surah 3.72 of the Qur'an.

scribes rarely signed their names to their work. As Van Der Toorn notes, the ancients' preoccupation was a work's *authority*, not its *authorship*.[33] For this reason, pseudepigraphy—the practice of writing a text in another's name, often a divine or legendary figure—was common in the ancient Near East, which ultimately gave rise to the practice in ancient Israelite and Jewish scribal culture.[34] Authors of biblical texts should, in most cases, be regarded as anonymous. One should not assume that Joshua was actually responsible for the composition of the book of Joshua just because the text was eventually called by his name. Nor should we assume that the person Job wrote the book of Job,[35] however much this may fly in the face of tradition. In the modern West, one occasionally encounters anonymous authorship in literature, and certain texts are composed under a pen name or written by a ghost writer, but in the main, books are generally composed by one writer to whom full credit is given. Such was not the norm in the ancient world.

Fourth, texts could exist in distinctly different versions because texts were fluid. *The Instruction of Shurrupag* was a fluid text that evolved over time and was eventually translated from the Sumerian language into Akkadian. Two distinct versions of *Gilgamesh and Huwawa* were part of a literary canon from Nibru.[36] Because of the numerous tablets of the Epic of Gilgamesh that have been discovered, we can know for certain that the Epic had an evolutionary history of approximately 1500 years, and if oral tradition is included, we are talking about roughly 2000 years.[37] If the evolutionary history of the Epic of

---

[33] Van Der Toorn, *Scribal Culture*, 27, 98.
[34] Person Jr., *The Deuteronomic History and the Book of Chronicles*, 50. For an overview of Old Testament pseudepigraphy, see Charlesworth, "Pseudepigrapha, OT," 537–540.
[35] See, e.g., b. B. Bathra 14b-15a.
[36] Black et al., *The Literature of Ancient Sumer*, xlix.
[37] Jacobsen, *The Treasures of Darkness*, 210.

Gilgamesh is taken as a model for the growth of biblical texts, the implications are considerable.[38]

Finally, there were no physical books in the ancient Near East, as least not in the way that we think of the modern book. Books today are made of numerous sheets of paper that are stacked, bound together, and covered. The ancient manuscript book, the "codex," did not exist until the first century CE, when it was adopted by early Christians, most likely, in Antioch.[39] Documents existed. Texts existed. Tablets and scrolls containing more than one text existed. Even canons existed (see, for example, the Sumerian scribal curricula).[40] But the codex was not used until perhaps shortly after Jesus' time, and it did not come into common use until the third century CE. In ancient Israel, texts were generally written on scrolls, which were made of sheets of parchment (animal skin) or papyrus (a predecessor of paper made from papyrus reeds), which were sown together and rolled up; and these scrolls were, to a certain extent, considered repositories in which more than one document could be recorded, as is clearly the case with the Psalter and Proverbs. This means, then, that in Jesus' time there was no Bible. There were scriptural texts, but it would be anachronistic to call them "biblical."

Conclusions

In this chapter, we have discovered that literacy was not a widespread phenomenon in ancient Near Eastern culture. This would suggest, then, that biblical texts were produced by those of elite status in ancient Israel, who were likely well connected with the palace and/or temple. We have also seen that the process of text production was fairly complicated, which means that it is not reasonable to suppose, as some conservative

---

[38]   See Tigay, "The Evolution of the Pentateuchal Narratives in the Light of the Evolution of the *Gilgamesh Epic*."

[39]   Roberts and Skeat, *The Birth of the Codex*, 58-61.

[40]   E.g., Black et al., *The Literature of Ancient Sumer*, 299-352.

thinkers do, that Hebrew Bible texts were each written by one author and passed down with little to no change. In order to demonstrate how most scholars view the process of biblical transmission, we will attempt in the next chapter to trace the history of the development of selected biblical books.

6
WHO WROTE THE BIBLE?

Moses wrote his own book and part of Balaam and Job. Joshua wrote the book that is called by his name and the last eight verses of the Torah. Samuel wrote the book that is called by his name and the book of Judges and Ruth. David wrote the book of Psalms, including in it the work of ten elders: Adam, Melchizedek, Abraham, Moses, Heman, Yeduthun, Asaph, and the three sons of Korah. Jeremiah wrote the book that is called by his name, the book of Kings, and Lamentations. Hezekiah and his colleagues wrote Isaiah, Proverbs, Song of Songs, and Qohelet. The Men of the Great Assembly wrote Ezekiel, the Twelve Minor Prophets, Daniel, and the scroll of Esther. Ezra wrote the book that is called by his name and the genealogies of the book of Chronicles up to his own time.

—b. Baba Bathra 14b-15a

In the last chapter, we learned about the following characteristics of ancient Near Eastern scribal culture: (1) authors were almost always anonymous, (2) texts were generally the products of communities, not individuals, and (3) books as we think of them today did not exist. Because of the considerable influence that ancient Near Eastern culture had on ancient Israelite culture, it should come as no surprise that the scribal culture of ancient Israel bore a striking resemblance to ancient Near Eastern scribal culture. While these three characteristics are inconsistent with traditional Judeo-Christian assumptions about how the texts of the Hebrew Bible were produced, we will see in this chapter that evidence from within the Hebrew Bible itself confirms that all three characteristics of ancient Near Eastern text production were also true for Israel.

Because we cannot examine the authorship of each book of the Hebrew Bible in this short chapter, we will consider a cross-section of the Hebrew Scriptures, three selected texts, one from each of the three major sections of the Hebrew Bible, to which scholars commonly appeal when they challenge traditional notions of biblical authorship. We will begin with the Psalter (i.e., the book of Psalms), our representative work from the Ketuvim, because it is fairly simple to demonstrate that it is the work of multiple authors. Building upon what we have learned from the Psalter, we will then look at Isaiah and the Torah.

The Psalter

According to tradition, David composed most of the psalms and was responsible for compiling his own work and the psalms of his predecessors and contemporaries, such as Moses (90:1), the sons of Korah (42:1), Asaph (50:1), and Solomon (72:1). Almost half of the Bible's 150 psalms are prefaced with "A Psalm of David" or a similar statement, so it is natural to see why many regard David as the author, at least of those works.[1] Furthermore, other passages within the Hebrew Bible indicate that David and many of Israel's leaders composed songs, a tradition that is reflected in the Targum of Song of Songs 1:1:[2]

> Songs and hymns that Solomon the prophet, the king of Israel, uttered in the spirit of holiness before the Master of All the World, the Lord. Ten songs have been uttered in the world, and this song is the most excellent of them all. **1.** Adam uttered the first song at the time when his sin was forgiven him and the Sabbath day came and protected him. He opened his mouth and said: A PSALM, A SONG for the Sabbath day... (Psalm 92:1). **2.** Moses uttered the second song with the children of Israel at the time when the Lord of Heaven split

---

[1]   See, for example, the first verse of Psalms 3-9.
[2]   For a discussion of the Aramaic Targumim, see chapter 7.

the Sea of Reeds. All of them opened their mouths together and uttered the song, which is thus written: THEN MOSES AND THE CHILDREN OF ISRAEL SANG... (Exodus 15:1). **3.** At the time when the well of water was given to them, the children of Israel uttered the third song, which is thus written: Then Moses and the children of Israel hymned (this) hymn... (Numbers 21:17). **4.** When his time came to depart from the world, Moses uttered the fourth song—and with it he admonished the people, the house of Israel—which is thus written: Hear, O Heavens, and I will speak... (Deuteronomy 32:1). **5.** Joshua son of Nun uttered the fifth song when he waged war in Gibeon and the sun and the moon stood still for him for thirty-six hours. And they stopped uttering (their own) song; he opened his mouth and uttered (his own) song, which is thus written: Thus Joshua hymned before the Lord... (Joshua 10:12). **6.** On the day when the Lord delivered over Sisera and his army into the hand of the children of Israel, Barak and Deborah uttered the sixth song, which is thus written: And Deborah and Barak son of Abinoam hymned... (Judges 5:1). **7.** At the time when a son was given to her from before the Lord, Hannah uttered the seventh song, which is thus written: And Hannah prayed in the spirit of prophecy... (1 Samuel 2:1). **8.** David the king of Israel uttered the eighth song because of every miracle that the Lord did for him. He opened his mouth and uttered a song, which is thus written: And David hymned in prophecy before the Lord... (2 Samuel 22:1). **9.** Solomon the king of Israel uttered the ninth song by the spirit of holiness before the Master of All the World, the Lord. **10.** At the time when they go out from their exile, the children of Israel will utter the tenth song, which is thus written and explained by Isaiah: This song will be for your joy as on the night that is sanctified for the festival of Passover, and (as) a joyful heart is in the people who go to appear before the Lord three times per year with all kinds of music and the sound of the drum while ascending the mountain of the Lord to worship before the Mighty One of Israel.[3]

---

[3]   Dost, "Song of Songs." I thank Roy Brown and Helen Brown of Accordance Bible Software for permission to include this lengthy excerpt.

Elsewhere in the Babylonian Talmud, we find evidence that at around the time of Jesus[4] it was believed that the Psalter in its entirety was David's song book:

> It has been taught on Tannaite authority: R. Meir would say, "All of the praises that are set forth in the book of Psalms did David recite, for it is said, 'The prayers of David son of Jesse are ended' (Psa. 72:20) — read not 'are ended' but 'all these.'"[5]

All of the foregoing is simply to say that the traditional belief that David compiled the book of Psalms is not baseless.

Nevertheless, when one carefully examines the Psalter's historical references, it is obvious that the version of the Psalter handed down to us could not possibly have reached its final form in David's time. This is perhaps clearest in Psalm 137. The first verse indicates that this psalm was written in Babylon as a lamentation over the loss of Jerusalem: "By the rivers of Babylon, there we sat down and wept as we remembered Zion." As the subsequent verses make clear, the community's lamentation concerns the destruction that Jerusalem and its inhabitants suffered at the hands of King Nebuchadnezzar II and his Babylonian army in 587/586 BCE, which culminated in a mass deportation to Babylon and the razing of the city and its temple (2 Kings 25:1-21). This is clear evidence that the Psalter

---

[4]   In the Talmud, to say that a teaching is based on "Tannaite authority" means that it was stated authoritatively by rabbis from the first to mid-third century CE, what is known as the "Tannaitic period." For an overview of the Tannaitic period, see Satlow, *Creating Judaism: History, Tradition, and Practice*, 115-39. It is important to note, however, that one cannot assume that any individual Talmudic tradition is historically reliable (Martín-Contreras and Miralles-Maciá, "Interdisciplinary Perspectives," 22).

[5]   B. Pesachim 117a (Neusner). The Hebrew form *klw* can mean "they are ended" (*kolluw*) or "all of it" (*kullow*). Here the Talmud follow an interpretation similar to the latter option by suggesting that the Hebrew text should be read *kol elu* ("all of these"). But as we see in printed versions of the Hebrew Bible, the vocalization of the Masoretes reflects the former interpretation.

was still a work in progress some four hundred years after David's time.

Furthermore, the statements taken as attributions of authorship, to which we made reference earlier, do not necessarily identify the authors of the psalms to which they are attached. For example, the Hebrew superscription[6] *ledavid* (לדוד) that introduces Psalm 25 does not necessarily mean that David wrote the psalm. The Hebrew form, which consists of the name "David" preceded by the preposition *le* (ל), can have any number of meanings, not all of which support Davidic authorship.[7] But regardless of how one interprets the superscription, scholars have detected that certain psalms attributed to David and other important individuals of Israel's early days are likely written long after the time of the purported authors.[8] According to Schmid, a great number of psalms are likely to be dated to the Persian era (late sixth century – late third century BCE), hundreds of years after the time of David. These psalms reflect theological interests of the period, particularly the universal dominion of

---

[6]   Here, the term "superscription" refers to text that is "written above" the main text.

[7]   Though see Kraus, *Psalms 1-59*, 22-23.

[8]   We run into the same issue in the New Testament. In *A Brief Introduction to the New Testament*, Ehrman considers seven of Paul's epistles to be "almost certainly" Pauline. Each of the other six are classified as "possibly pseudonymous" and "probably pseudonymous" (183). Elsewhere, he argues that every New Testament document may be characterized as "orthonymous," "homonymous," or "pseudonymous." Orthonymous works are those that are attributed to the true author, as is the case of Paul's letter to the Romans, for example. Others, like Revelation, may have been written by someone with the same name as the traditional author, while other works are pseudonymous, or written under a name other than the author's true name. Pseudonymous works, according to Ehrman, may be incorrectly ascribed to an individual either because the true author wishes to use a pen name or because (s)he wishes to imbue the work with authority by using an authoritative figure's name. The latter case is what Ehrman calls "forgery" (Ehrman, *Forged: Writing in the Name of God—Why the Bible's Authors Are not Who We Think They Are*, 22-24).

Israel's God,[9] which is characteristic of many of the clearly later texts of the Hebrew Scriptures, such as Daniel.[10]

Schmid also argues that the Psalter had not yet reached its final (or "crystallized") form by the beginning of the Persian period. This can be inferred from the existence of a collection of forty-two psalms within the Psalter (Psalms 42-83) known as the "Elohistic Psalter."[11] The Elohistic Psalter is distinguished by the use of "Elohim," the Hebrew word for "God," which is really more of a title, instead of God's name "Yahweh" (commonly referred to as the "Tetragrammaton," God's four-letter name). A number of psalms within this corpus have parallels elsewhere in the Psalter. For instance, Psalm 53 is almost identical to Psalm 14, but whereas Psalm 14 uses the Tetragrammaton, Psalm 53 uses *elohim*:

14:2 **Yahweh** has looked down from heaven on the children of man to see: Is there one who is wise, who seeks **Yahweh**?

53:3 **God** has looked down from heaven on the children of man to see: Is there one who is wise, who seeks **God**?

Psalm 14:4, 7 are similarly modified in Psalm 53.[12] The practice of refraining from writing God's name becomes increasingly characteristic in the postexilic period (as we shall discuss in more detail in chapter 7), which is evidence that the Elohistic redaction of these psalms took place at a fairly late date.

But more than this, the Psalms scrolls from Qumran (where most of the Dead Sea Scrolls were found) preserve a Psalter whose arrangement is not fixed. Within the Psalms scrolls are attested five distinct arrangements of Psalm 91

9   Schmid, *The Old Testament: A Literary History*, 152-53.
10   See, e.g., Daniel 2:37; 7:27
11   Schmid, *The Old Testament*, 153-54.
12   For additional examples, see Limburg, "Psalms, Book of," 526.

through the end of the Psalter.[13] This indicates that the Psalter was still in a state of flux in the final centuries prior to the Common Era.

From our brief discussion of the Psalter we have learned that:

1. The superscriptions to many psalms suggest that David cannot have been the only one to have contributed to the Psalter. However, if we were to understand *ledavid* as an affirmation of Davidic authorship, then we would have to assume that Moses, Asaph, Solomon, and the many others mentioned in the various superscriptions must have also played a role in the development of the Psalter. Either way, the Psalter must be regarded as the work of more than one author.

2. There is reason to believe that at least some of the psalms attributed to David were actually composed long after his time.

3. Some psalms have been considered to be adaptations of non-Israelite psalms. In chapter 4, we saw that this was the case with Psalm 29, and this is how Albright viewed Psalm 68, a view that is ostensibly consistent with the early Hebrew of the psalm.

4. Some psalms were revised well after the date of their composition, as we saw with the Elohistic Psalter. And Gunkel contends that Psalm 68, for whatever its early origins, shows evidence of postexilic editing.[14] This indicates that the Psalter is not only the work of various authors but also various editors, as is the case with other

---

[13] Abegg, Jr. et al., *The Dead Sea Scrolls Bible: The Oldest Known Bible Translated for the First Time into English*, 507.

[14] For a discussion of the history of Psalm 68 scholarship, see Kraus, *Psalms 60-150*, 47-51.

ancient Near Eastern documents, such as the Epic of Gilgamesh.

What we have learned about the Psalter's transmission history is clearly true of other works in the Ketuvim. A number of the Writings appear to have a similar transmission history. Editorial comments in Proverbs, for instance, demarcate collections within the "book."[15] And judging from the shift in tone, style, and theology, many scholars are of the opinion that the final six verses of Ecclesiastes almost surely belong to at least one additional writer.[16] And like the writer of Psalm 29 and the redactors of the Psalter, the writer(s) of Chronicles drew from and incorporated earlier sources. We must conclude, then, that the transmission of the Ketuvim was quite complex. And we will see from our discussion of Isaiah, to which we now turn, that there is overwhelming evidence that such is also the case with the Prophets.

Isaiah

It would seem that the book of Isaiah was already understood to have been authored by the eighth-century figure Isaiah of Jerusalem by the time the New Testament was written. According to the Acts of the Apostles 8:27-33, Isaiah 53:7-8 is part of what was simply known as "Isaiah." The introductory formulae found at the beginning of the text's first and second chapters are the principal reason that this sixty-six chapter text is attributed to him:

---

[15] Proverbs 1:1; 10:1; 22:17; 24:23; 25:1; 30:1; 31:1.

[16] For a discussion of the various readings of Ecclesiastes 12:9-14, see Krüger, *Qoheleth*, 208-9; Seow, *Ecclesiastes*, 391-96. It is important to keep in mind, however, that determining a date for Ecclesiastes is fraught with complexity (Carr, *The Formation of the Hebrew Bible*, 448-55).

1:1 The vision of Isaiah son of Amoz, which he saw concerning Judah and Jerusalem in the days of Uzziah, Jotham, Ahaz, and Hezekiah, kings of Judah.

2:1 The matter[17] that Isaiah son of Amoz saw concerning Judah and Jerusalem.

And in Isaiah 8:1, 16, we find evidence that Isaiah and those in his circle could write and did write. So, it is understandable why this biblical text is commonly understood to be the product of Isaiah of Jerusalem.[18]

However, one does not need to read very far into the book of Isaiah to find evidence that scribes who lived centuries after Isaiah of Jerusalem had a hand in supplementing the eighth-century work. The two chapters that immediately follow the so-called Isaian Diary, the book's first major section (Isaiah 1-12),[19] are not concerned principally with Assyria, the empire in whose shadow Israel and Judah dwelled during the eighth century and most of the seventh century, but with Babylon (see Isa 13:1, 19; 14:4, 22), an empire that did not govern Judah until well over a century had passed from the time of Isaiah's call to prophesy. Furthermore, Isaiah 40-66 never mentions Isaiah of Jerusalem and there is only one reference to Assyria (Isa 52:4), which presents Assyria as just as much of a memory as the Egypt of the Exodus.

Since the late nineteenth century, many biblical scholars have seen fit to divide Isaiah into three sections: First Isaiah (1-39), Second Isaiah (40-55),[20] and Third Isaiah (56-66).[21] First Isaiah contains eighth-century material, but it also contains later material from various periods. The aforementioned oracles

---

[17] Or "word."

[18] This perspective is presented at the opening of Mel Gibson's 2004 film, "The Passion of the Christ," which opens with a partial quotation of Isaiah 53:5 followed by the date of 700 BC.

[19] Ginsberg, "Reflexes of Sargon after 715 BCE," 43.

[20] Also known as "Deutero-Isaiah."

[21] Also known as "Trito-Isaiah."

against Babylon together constitute one clear example, and the virtually verbatim transfer of 2 Kings 18-20 into the Isaiah scroll likewise indicates that this biblical text, like the Psalter, continued to develop long after the lifetime of the original author.[22] Isaiah 24-27 may be among the last units to be added to the Isaiah scroll, because, as Blenkinsopp notes, certain features of this section may be understood as references to the Seleucid and Ptolemaic periods, which followed the death of Alexander the Great in 323 BCE.[23]

There is little doubt that Second Isaiah (Isaiah 40-55) dates to sometime after the end of Babylonian rule (539 BCE) because of its praise for the Persian conqueror of Babylon, Cyrus the Great (Isaiah 44:28; 45:1), who, according to a number of biblical passages, was favorable toward the people of Israel.[24] Some religiously conservative thinkers are inclined to view Isaiah 44:28 and 45:1 as *predictions* of Cyrus. But such explanations are not based on a careful reading of the text, which reveals that the author personally knows of Cyrus. Furthermore, they fail to realize that ancient Israelite prophets were not in the habit of predicting by name the coming of any individual.[25] That prophets are primarily foretellers, predicting events long before they occur, is a popular view of Israelite prophecy. However, more often than not, the biblical prophets concern themselves with *forth*-telling the words of God. The book of Amos, for example, which is one of the earliest of the written prophetic works, does not predict in detail the imminent Assyrian invasion and exile.[26] The prediction in which the early material within the

---

[22]   For an excellent summary of these issues, see Blenkinsopp, *A History of Prophecy in Israel* (rev. ed.), 98-100.

[23]   Ibid., 239.

[24]   E.g., Daniel 6:28; Ezra 6:14.

[25]   Most scholars consider the Hebrew Bible's few examples of this phenomenon as *vaticinia ex eventu* ("prophecy after the fact").

[26]   During the period of the Syro-Ephraimite conflict of ca. 733 (see 2 Kings 16 and Isaiah 7) through the destruction of the Northern Kingdom in 722, the Assyrian emperors Tiglath-pileser III and Shalmaneser V inflicted Israel with carnage, destruction, and, at least politically speaking, extinction.

book of Amos engages is of a more general nature. Typically, those who argue that these prophetic texts are not composite works (i.e., works composed from distinct, independent parts) do so not because of available evidence but because of their ideology and mistaken notions of what ancient Israelite prophecy is and is not.

Third Isaiah is generally dated even later because ideologically it reflects the period of the late sixth century BCE and beyond, though it may contain some earlier material.[27] Blenkinsopp sees indications of an early Persian period setting in Isaiah 66:1-5 because the text, in his opinion, shows evidence of a division within the Judaism of Palestine involving a group that identified with the teachings of the so-called "servant songs" of Isaiah 49; 50, 52-53.[28]

Another compelling line of evidence that supports later dating for Isaiah 40-66 is the presence of inner-biblical interpretation. Zakovitch defines inner-biblical interpretation as:

> the light that one biblical text casts onto another – whether to solve a problem within the interpreted text or to adapt the interpreted text to the beliefs and ideas of the interpreter. The interpreting text may stand far from the interpreted text, or be next to it, or may even be incorporated within it. Not always does a text function solely as the interpreting or as the

---

Though this watershed period was within only a generation of Amos' preaching against the Northern Kingdom, neither of these figures nor the dates of their coming is foretold. For a careful treatment of the growth of the book of Amos, see Barton, *The Theology of the Book of Amos.*

The Hebrew Bible contains different types of eschatological ("end-times") prophecy. Pre-exilic prophecy is not at all apocalyptic in nature; it is not interested in the end of human history but the imminent end of the current world system. Later Israelite prophecy becomes increasingly broader in its temporal scope. For a brief survey of the periods of Israelite prophecy, see the relevant *ABD* articles.

[27] Blenkinsopp, *A History of Prophecy in Ancient Israel,*183.
[28] Ibid., 220.

interpreted one: sometimes the two will mutually interpret one another.[29]

Most avid Bible readers are aware that inner-biblical interpretation occurs elsewhere in the Hebrew Bible, even if they do not refer to it by this name. For example, Daniel 9:2 interprets Jeremiah's prophecy of the seventy years (Jeremiah 25:11-12; 29:10), which was written over four hundred years earlier:

> In the first year of his reign, I Daniel considered in the Scriptures the number of years that the word of the Lord had revealed to the prophet Jeremiah for the completion of the desolation of Jerusalem, seventy years.

Because seventy years had long since come and gone by the time that Daniel 9 was being written, and the people had already returned to the land, just as Jeremiah had said, why would the writer of Daniel have wrestled with the meaning of Jeremiah's prophecy? The reason is that an interpretive tradition had developed according to which the word of God was believed to bear multiple levels of meaning. Texts that were regarded as sacred came to be characterized as "omnisignificant," as Kugel puts it.[30] This approach to sacred texts goes back at least to 721 BCE, when refugees from the Northern Kingdom of Israel fled south toward Jerusalem as a result of the Assyrian invasion, and brought their sacred texts with them. Texts such as Hosea and Amos were reinterpreted at that time, and their messages were

---

[29]   Zakovitch, "Inner-Biblical Interpretation," 92. Two important works that explore this process in some detail are Michael Fishbane's *Biblical Interpretation in Ancient Israel* (1989) and Yair Zakovitch's *An Introduction to Inner-Biblical Interpretation* (1992, Hebrew). Both of these works offer insightful proposals into where, how, and why tensions arose within the biblical corpus. Even if one rejects one point or another, the overall body of evidence warrants our taking a fresh look at how the biblical corpus developed over the course of the first millennium BCE.

[30]   Kugel, *The Bible as It Was*, 21.

applied to Israel's southern neighbor, Judah.[31] In other words, this non-contextual approach to the Hebrew Scriptures is at least as old as Isaiah of Jerusalem.

The book of Isaiah itself is a repository for inner-biblical interpretation. And interestingly, Sommer argues that Isaiah 40-66 more closely resemble the contents of Jeremiah than Isaiah.[32] But regardless, what we find is that according to the writers of Isaiah 40-66, the prophets of old were now read as heralds of events that were to take place centuries after them. This view of prophecy took root in Judaism (and later in Christianity), as the Isaiah Targum (ca. fourth century CE) attests in 41:27:

> The words of comfort that the prophets prophesied from of old concerning Zion, behold, they have come. I will provide a proclaimer for Jerusalem.

This means that prophets such as Amos, Hosea, Micah, and Isaiah came to be understood as speaking not only of events that pertain to their immediate audience, but to subsequent generations, as well. The words of the prophets were now understood to possess a depth of meaning extending far beyond their historical, contextual meaning. And as we will see in chapter 8, this is precisely the reason that Matthew 2:15 interprets as a messianic prophecy a statement from Hosea 11:1 that clearly refers not to the future but to the past.

So far, we have seen that both the Psalter and Isaiah, like many other books in the Prophets and the Writings, were composed by numerous writers over the course of many centuries. We turn our attention now to the Torah, which has traditionally been understood to be the work of Moses, to see if it too is actually a composite work.

---

[31] Blenkinsopp, *History of Prophecy*, 78; Jeremias, *The Book of Amos*, 5-9; Schmid, *The Old Testament: A Literary History*, 90. For a detailed but somewhat less technical treatment of the development of the book of Amos, see Barton, *The Theology of the Book of Amos*.

[32] Sommer, *A Prophet Reads Scripture*, 106.

The Torah/Pentateuch

Almost annually, I teach a course on the Pentateuch to Christian seminary students. As is the custom in most of the other courses that I teach, we begin by examining our presuppositions. Of the many questions that we consider in the first week, the one in which students are most interested is the question of authorship. The operating assumption of almost every student in the class is that Moses wrote the Torah, except, perhaps, for the final chapter (Deuteronomy 34), which recounts the circumstances of his death. Some assume that even this material was revealed to Moses by God in advance, since Moses is regarded as a prophet (e.g., Exodus 3-6).

Numerous passages in the Hebrew Bible and in the New Testament appear to confirm this assumption.[33] Take, for instance, Joshua 8:30-32:

> Then Joshua built an altar to the LORD, the God of Israel, on Mt. Ebal, just as Moses, the servant of the LORD, commanded the children of Israel, according to that which is written in the scroll of Moses' instruction: "An altar of whole stones that iron (tools) have not struck." And they offered upon it burnt offerings to the LORD, and they sacrificed sacrifices of well-being. And there they wrote upon stones a copy of Moses' instruction, which he himself had written before the children of Israel.

---

[33] The following is a selection of verses from all three sections of the Hebrew Bible and the New Testament:

Torah: Exodus 17:14; 24:4; 34:1, 27-28; 39:30; Numbers 5:23; 17:2-3; 33:2; Deuteronomy 4:13; 5:22; 6:9; 10:2, 4; 11:20; 17:18; 27:3, 8; 31:9, 19, 22.

Prophets: Joshua 1:1-8; 8:31-32; 1 Kings 2:3; 8:9; 2 Kings 14:6; 23:25.

Writings: Daniel 9:13; Ezra 7:6; 8:1, 14; 2 Chronicles 23:18; 25:4.

New Testament: Mark 12:19; Luke 16:29; 24:27, 44; John 1:45; 7:22-23; Acts 15:21; 21:21; 26:22; 28:23; Romans 10:5, 19; 1 Corinthians 9:9; 2 Corinthians 3:15; Hebrews 10:8.

According to this passage, Joshua builds the altar to Israel's God in accordance with Deuteronomy 27:4-6:

> Now when you cross the Jordan you are to erect these stones, (concerning) which I command you today, on Mt. Ebal. And you will build an altar of whole stones; you will not strike them with iron (tools). With whole stone you will build the altar of the LORD, your God. And you will offer upon them burnt offerings to the LORD, your God.

Thus, while Joshua 8:30-31 is not a verbatim quotation of its source, it does present itself as preserving the very voice of Moses.[34] This is just one of numerous examples in the Hebrew Scriptures that many Bible readers understandably take as evidence for Mosaic authorship of the Torah.

Likewise, many New Testament passages ostensibly support the notion of Mosaic authorship of the Torah. Take, for instance, Matthew 19:7-8, part of Jesus' exchange with some Pharisees concerning the morality of divorce:

> They said to him, "Why, then, did Moses command to give a bill of divorce and to divorce her?" Jesus said to them, "Moses allowed you to divorce your wives because of your hard hearts, but from the beginning it was not so."

It would seem, according to Matthew, that both Jesus and the Pharisees share a perspective similar to b. Baba Bathra 14b-15a, which affirms Mosaic authorship of the Torah.

The most recent work of scholarship of which I am aware that defends Mosaic authorship of the Torah is Sailhamer's *The Meaning of the Pentateuch: Revelation, Composition, and Interpretation*, in which he argues that the Pentateuch existed in two principal versions in antiquity. The first is the "Mosaic

---

[34] New Testament scholars debate to what extent the Gospels' quotations of Jesus preserve the very words of Jesus (Lat. *ipsissima verba*) or the very voice of Jesus (Lat. *ipsissima vox*).

Pentateuch," which, as the name suggests, was written by Moses himself. The second is the "Prophetic Pentateuch," which included messianic commentary, such as Deuteronomy 34.[35] Sailhamer argues from biblical evidence that Moses wrote the first Pentateuch and that the second and final Pentateuch was written much later but was unlikely much different from Pentateuch 1.0.[36] There is, then, little to distinguish Sailhamer's conclusions from common presuppositions based on a cursory reading of a modern translation of the Pentateuch.[37]

It is important to note, however, that reading the text closely has led others to very different conclusions about the Pentateuch's origins and development. In the twelfth century CE, Abraham Ben Meir Ibn Ezra (henceforth, "Ibn Ezra") made significant advances in contextual (Heb. *peshat*) exegesis of the Hebrew Scriptures. Guided by grammar and reason, his contextual reading of the Torah led him to conclusions about the Torah's origins that were fundamentally different from those held by rabbinic Judaism.[38] His methodological commitment to reading the Bible contextually led him to the conclusion that scribes living long after the time of Moses helped to shape the Torah. In his oft-quoted commentary on Deuteronomy 1:2, he writes:

> And if you understand the secret of the twelve – as well as "And Moses wrote" (Deuteronomy 31:22), "And the Canaanites were then in the land" (Genesis 12:6), "On the mountain of the LORD it will be seen" (Genesis 22:14), and

---

35 Sailhamer, *The Meaning of the Pentateuch*, 17.
36 Ibid., 24
37 This is not surprising, as many of the sources that he cites are very dated, and he chooses not to engage with and build upon more recent developments in the field.
38 Simon, "Jewish Exegesis in Spain and Provence, and in the East, in the Twelfth and Thirteenth Centuries," 378-79. It should be noted the Christian exegesis is also traditionally non-contextual, as we will see in chapter 8.

"Behold, his bed was a bed of iron" (Deuteronomy 3:11) – you understand the truth.

The "secret of the twelve" refers to the last twelve verses of Deuteronomy, which, as we noted above, record the death of Moses, something about which he could not have written. Likewise, the other biblical passages to which Ibn Ezra refers could not possibly have been composed by Moses either because they speak of the time of Moses as past. Given what we have learned about the Psalter and Isaiah, this should come as no surprise.

Ibn Ezra's insights did not begin to substantively transform the common perception of the Torah's origin for half of a millennium. But approximately five hundred years after Ibn Ezra wrote his commentary on Deuteronomy, the Jewish-Dutch philosopher Baruch (Benedict) Spinoza unabashedly spelled out in detail what Ibn Ezra had previously stated only cryptically. After presenting the portion presented above, Spinoza writes:

> In these few words he hints, and also shows that it was not Moses who wrote the Pentateuch, but someone who lived long after him, and further, that the book which Moses wrote was something different from any now extant.[39]

He then proceeds to unpack this revelation, leaving the reader in no doubt of his position. Now while Spinoza was writing on this issue in the Netherlands, Simon and Hobbes were coming to similar conclusions in France and England, respectively. Over the course of the next three centuries, a consensus began to develop that Moses could not have been responsible for the composition of the Pentateuch. This culminated with Julius Wellhausen's *Prolegomena to the History of Ancient Israel* (1883), which identified four literary sources—J, E, D, and P— that show, according to Wellhausen, the evolution and

---

[39]   Spinoza, *A Theologico-Political Treatise*, 121.

devolution of Israelite religion.[40] Even though major developments in this field of research have occurred since this time, Wellhausen's "Documentary Hypothesis" has left an indelible impression on biblical scholars down to the present.

We need to be clear, though, that it is not merely on the basis of the few minor details found in Ibn Ezra's statement that scholarship has abandoned the notion of Mosaic authorship. And it is more than just the different stages of biblical Hebrew present in the Torah (see chapter 2) that suggest a lengthy compositional process. There are at least ten different characteristic features of the Torah, all of which are covered widely in the scholarly literature, that have given rise to the scholarly consensus.[41]

***

Ultimately, these insights compel scholars to read Psalms, Isaiah, and the Torah as ancient Near Eastern texts that underwent a complex editorial history, as one should expect of ancient Near Eastern texts. Traditionally, it has been assumed that each biblical book belongs to one author in the same way that modern books generally have one author. But evidence put forward by modern scholarship suggests that the Torah, Isaiah, and Psalms in their present forms may have developed from a number of oral and written sources that were redacted and woven together over time. The transmission of some Hebrew Bible texts may have been a simpler process, as some argue is the case with Ecclesiastes;[42] but simplicity is the exception, not the rule.

---

[40]   For a brief introduction to Simon and Hobbes, and the subsequent scholars who paved the way for Wellhausen, see Ska, *Introduction to Reading the Pentateuch*, 101-12. For careful analysis of Wellhausen's *Prolegomena* vis-à-vis Kauffman's influential rebuttal, see Geller, "Wellhausen and Kauffman."

[41]   See Friedman, "Torah (Pentateuch)," 605–622.

[42]   E.g., see Krüger, *Qoheleth*, 208-9; Seow, *Ecclesiastes*, 391-96.

In my experience, many who come from more conservative religious backgrounds are distrustful of the type of scholarship discussed in this chapter and the individuals who conduct it. Such is "the wisdom of man," I have often heard it said. But any reconstruction of the Bible's development, however simple or complex, conservative or otherwise, is based on interpretation of available evidence. All wisdom, including conservative wisdom, is, in the end, "man's wisdom." While no one agrees on all of the particulars of when and by whom the texts comprising the Hebrew Bible were written, current research demonstrates convincingly that the Hebrew Bible's transmission history was more complex than most assume, and this knowledge has profoundly impacted what is known about how the Hebrew Bible became a book.

7

THE BIBLE IN TRANSLATION, PART 1
THE ARAMAIC TARGUMS

*And they read aloud from God's Instruction with translation
and explanation so that the people could understand the
Scripture.*

—Nehemiah 8:8

The first millennium BCE was a time of great change for the
people of Israel. Some of the change was geographical in nature.
The Assyrian Exile (eighth century) and the Babylonian Exile
(sixth century) involved the deportation of countless individuals
from Israel and Judah to Mesopotamia, only some of whom
would later return. The people of Israel became a geographically
diasporic[1] people, which means that God had become a
geographically diasporic God. But change in geography brings
with it change in culture. The exile to Babylon was just as much
of a cultural exile as it was a geographical one. The end of
temple worship and its concomitant animal sacrifice, as well as
the rise of synagogue worship[2] and the substitution of prayer for

---

[1]   The term "diaspora" and the corresponding adjective "diasporic"
refer to groups who are separate, whether in terms of location or culture.

[2]   This is reflected in Ezekiel, in which God leaves his home,
Jerusalem's temple (Ezekiel 10), and relocates to Babylon, where his people
must now worship him in a very different way. Temple worship was no
longer possible (at least until the rebuilding of the temple in the early
postexilic period), which may have led to an early form of synagogue worship
(Ezekiel 11:16; we should note, however, this is not a foregone conclusion
[Cohen, *From the Maccabees to the Mishnah*, 107]).

94 Jesus' Bible

sacrifice[3] to their *ostensibly* defeated God,[4] radically transformed Israel's religion. And the allure of Babylonian religion and culture coupled with the advantages that stem from assimilating[5] naturally granted inroads to Babylonian paganism among the Israelite and Judean expatriates. Therefore, those who wished to remain faithful to their God and his Torah needed to become a culturally diasporic people.[6]

The people were not only culturally diasporic in terms of their religion. Living in Mesopotamia meant that, willingly or not, they would slowly lose their proficiency in Hebrew and would acclimate to Aramaic, the spoken language of their new land. As their children and grandchildren grew up speaking Aramaic and used it in the marketplace and in business,[7] the Hebrew that they spoke in Judea would become decreasingly familiar, as would the Classical Hebrew of the Scriptures.

This is perfectly understandable when we consider that native speakers of modern Hebrew commonly misunderstand aspects of biblical Hebrew texts because the grammar and syntax have evolved and many words have either changed in meaning or have been replaced with new words. For instance, the word *hashmal* (חַשְׁמָל) means "electricity" in modern Hebrew, but in Ezekiel 1:16 it means something like "electrum." This is something that an Israeli is not likely to know unless it has come up in the course of religious training.[8]

---

3   This language occurs in psalms 50; 107 & 116. For evidence of the lateness of these psalms, see Kraus, *Psalms 1-59*, 490, 496-97; *Psalms 60-150*, 330-31; 386.

4   Deijl, *Protest or Propaganda: War in the Old Testament book of Kings and in Contemporaneous Ancient Near Eastern Texts*, 663.

5   See Ezekiel 14.

6   See our discussion of Genesis 1 on pages 53-58.

7   Lukko & Buylaere, "Languages and Writing Systems in Assyria," 318-19.

8   This is not much different from how poorly modern American English speakers comprehend the Early Modern English of Shakespeare or the King James Bible (see Nevalainen, *An Introduction to Early Modern English*). Some of the changes sound strange to the modern ear but are

Aramaic texts from Egypt and the Fertile Crescent[9] dating to the middle of the first millennium BCE suggest that Israelite and Judean exiles would have spoken and understood Aramaic. And from this period, we have evidence that (1) Aramaic script replaced Hebrew script in the writing of Hebrew, (2) Aramaic terms were used in Palestine, (3) Babylonian month names were adopted by Israelites,[10] and (4) Akkadian terms came into Hebrew through Aramaic.[11] Thus, the language and writing system of the exiled and non-exiled people of Israel would have been drastically transformed over the course of the sixth century BCE.

In the Persian period, Aramaic became the administrative language of what was now the province of Yehud,[12] and the older Hebrew of the Torah would no longer have been understood by many of those living in Yehud in the early Persian era.[13] This is most evident in Nehemiah 8:1-8, the account of Ezra's public recitation of the Torah:[14]

[1]And all the people gathered as one person to the public square that was by the Water Gate. They told Ezra the scribe to bring the scroll of Moses' Instruction, which God commanded Israel.

---

nevertheless intelligible, as in "Our Father which art in Heaven," (ibid., 5.) but many of even the most regular Bible readers cannot accurately explain in plain modern English the meaning of the statement "Hallowed be thy name" (Matthew 6:9, KJV). And this is to say nothing of such archaic English words and expressions as "bewrayeth" (Proverbs 27:16), "wot" (Genesis 21:26), "habergeon" (Exodus 28:32), "lucre" (1 Samuel 8:3), "doleful creatures" (Isaiah 13:21), and "peradventure" (Genesis 18:24).

[9]   "Fertile Crescent" refers to the area from the Persian Gulf to Israel and Palestine.

[10]   Y. Rosh Hashanah 1:56a.

[11]   Schniedewind, *A Social History of Hebrew*, 134.

[12]   "Yehud" is related to the Hebrew term for "Judah," which is *yehuda*.

[13]   Likewise, Schniedewind, *A Social History of Hebrew*, 141.

[14]   Scholars have not been able to confidently determine the time of Ezra's presence in Yehud, with suggestions ranging from the mid-fifth century BCE through the early-fourth century BCE (Leith, "Israel among the Nations: The Persian Period," 281).

[2]So on the first day of the seventh month, Ezra the priest brought the Instruction before the congregation, consisting of men, women, and all who could understand what they heard. [3]He read from it before the public square that was by the Water Gate, from morning until midday before the men, the women, and all who could understand. The ears of all the people were attentive to the scroll of the Instruction. [4]Ezra the scribe stood on a wooden platform that they brought for this purpose. And Mattithiah, Shema, Anaiah, Uriah, Hilkiah, and Maaseiah stood beside him, at his right hand; and to his left were Pedaiah, Mishael, Malchijah, Hashum, Hashbaddanah, Zechariah, and Meshullam. [5]Ezra the scribe opened the scroll in the sight of all the people, for he was stationed above all of the people. As he opened it, all the people stood. [6]Ezra praised the LORD, the greatest God, and all the people responded, "Amen, Amen," while raising their hands. And they bowed down and prostrated themselves on the ground before the LORD. [7]Meanwhile, Yeshua, Bani, Sherebiah, Jamin, Akkub, Shabbethai, Hodiah, Maaseiah, Kelita, Azariah, Jozabad, Hanan, Pelaiah, the Levites, were explaining the Instruction to the people, while the people stood in attendance. [8]And they read aloud from God's Instruction with translation and explanation so that the people could understand the Scripture.

It would appear that to the people in attendance, much of what Ezra read from the Torah scroll would have been unintelligible due to their lack of familiarity with Hebrew grammar and vocabulary, and perhaps even the broader context and the interpretive techniques according to which the religious leaders read the text. For this reason, the Hebrew text was translated into Aramaic and interpreted for the people as Ezra read.

Over time, translating the Scriptures into Aramaic in the synagogue became a part of the liturgy. According to the Jerusalem Talmud, Nehemiah 8 is the foundation for this synagogue custom:

How do we know from Scripture that there is to be a translation of the biblical readings for the congregation? R.

Zeirah in the name of R. Hanan: "['And they read from the book, from the law of God, clearly; and they gave the sense, so that the people understood the reading' (Neh. 8:8).] 'And they read from the book, from the law of God' — this refers to the Scripture. "'Clearly' — this refers to the translation thereof. "'And they gave the sense' — this refers to the proper articulation. "'So that the people understood the reading' — this refers to the tradition [on the meaning]."[15]

The expectation was that the translator would provide not a literal translation (Aram. *targum*; pl. *targumim*) but a dynamic translation through which the meaning of the text would be accurately conveyed to the congregation. From rabbinic evidence we learn that the translations were expected to be improvised and non-literal.[16] The Palestinian targumic tradition is very free, in fact, as we will see below in our discussion of Targums Neofiti and Pseudo-Jonathan. But as it turned out, the more literal translation, Targum Onqelos, became the official Aramaic translation of the Torah and the one canonized in the rabbinic Bible.[17]

What is the earliest evidence for written Targums? The Babylonian Talmud refers to a Targum of Job, which was in existence by the first century CE,[18] but we know from the Dead Sea Scrolls that Targums of both Job (4Q157 / 4QtgJob and 11Q10 / 11QtgJob) and at least part of Leviticus (4Q156 / 4QtgLev) had already been produced in the last pre-Christian centuries.[19] The latter consists of only two small fragments of Leviticus 16:12-15 and 16:18-21 dating to the second or first century BCE. In his presentation of Kasher's notes on these two fragments, Milik observes that while these two fragments are to

---

[15]   Y. Megilloth 4:1 (Neusner). See also m. Meg 2:1.

[16]   Elbogen, *Jewish Liturgy: A Comprehensive History*,152.

[17]   Some Jews still read the weekly Torah portion twice in Hebrew and Onqelos' translation once.

[18]   B. Shabbat 155a.

[19]   For transcription and translation of these texts, see García Martínez & Tigchelaar, *Dead Sea Scrolls Study Edition*, 302-305, 1184-1201.

be understood as distinct from the later Targumim (see below), they are not simply literal translations; they preserve elements of oral Torah.[20]

The Targum of Job from Qumran cave 4 (4QtgJob), contains fragments of Job 3-5, which is a highly literal translation of a Hebrew *Vorlage*[21] (i.e., the original text from which a translation is produced) that is similar to or identical to the Masoretic Text. The Targum of Job from cave 11 (11QtgJob), which shows evidence of having been written by a different scribe,[22] may date to 150-100 BCE.[23] It is a simple translation, but one that regularly paraphrases, perhaps because the Hebrew of Job is often difficult to interpret.[24]

"Targums" in the formal sense, however, refers to a corpus of expansive Aramaic translations that date from the early rabbinic period, perhaps as early as the first century CE, to perhaps as late as the twelfth century CE.[25] Targum Onqelos, which is the most literal of the Targums of the Torah, is the earliest. Its first version dates to between the first century CE and the middle of the second century CE. The youngest of the three Targums of the Torah, Pseudo-Jonathan, dates to the early-

---

[20]   Stuckenbruck and Freedman, "The Fragments of a Targum to Leviticus in Qumran Cave 4 (4Q156): A Linguistic Comparison and Assessment," 94-95. Milik, "Notes by Menaḥem M. Kasher on the Fragments of Targum to Leviticus and the Commentary," 93.

[21]   Pronounced *FOHR-lah-guh*.

[22]   Vasholz, "4QTargumJob versus 11QTargum Job," 109.

[23]   Sokoloff, *11QTgJob*, 9. Similarly, Kaufman, "The Job Targum from Qumran," 317-18. Muraoka, however, is inclined to date it to 250-150 BCE (Muraoka, "The Aramaic of the Old Targum of Job from Qumran Cave XI," 443).

[24]   Kaufman, "The Job Targum from Qumran," 317-18.

[25]   The most comprehensive, up-to-date translation of the Targumim is the series *The Aramaic Bible: The Targums*, published by Liturgical Press. This series is a critical English-language edition of the Targumim and a fine work of scholarship that makes the Targumim accessible to broader scholarship and non-specialists alike. Accordance Bible Software, however, has recently published electronically a new translation of the Targumim, which is more affordable and accessible than the Liturgical Press series.

to mid-fifth century CE. The Palestinian Targums date to somewhere in between Onqelos and Pseudo-Jonathan.[26] Targum Jonathan of the Prophets dates to somewhere around the fourth century CE,[27] and the individual Targums of the Writings date from the time of Pseudo-Jonathan on into the Islamic period.

Characteristics of the Targums

As we have already noted, the Targums are "expansive" translations of the Hebrew Scriptures. However, some Targums are more expansive than others. The three principle Targums of the Torah differ significantly in this regard. Onqelos, the oldest of the three, is the least expansive, and Pseudo-Jonathan, which is the youngest, exhibits the greatest degree of expansiveness, though the degree of expansiveness within each Targum varies from

Figure 4: An excerpt containing Deuteronomy 5:6-7 from a 14th-century manuscript (JTS MS L127, SHF 1397:2) in which every verse from the Torah is followed by Targum Onqelos' translation. Image courtesy of the Library of the Jewish Theological Seminary.

verse to verse. An examination of the three Targums' treatment of Genesis 22:1 provides a glimpse of how differently the Targums can render a single verse.

---

26   Chilton and Flesher, *The Targums: A Critical Introduction*, 158-59.
27   Chilton and Flesher note that every passage in the Talmud in which the Aramaic of the Prophets is quoted is attributed to the fourth-century Joseph bar Hiyya (Ibid., 173.) For this reason, they conclude that Targum Jonathan was redacted in the fourth century CE.

Masoretic Text
Now it happened after these things that God tested Abraham.
And he said to him, "Abraham." And he said, "Here I am."

Onqelos
Now it happened after these things that the LORD tested
Abraham. And he said to him, "Abraham." And he said, "Here
I am."

Onqelos' translation of the Hebrew is very literal. The only
way in which it differs is by its substituting out "God" in
favor of "the LORD."

Neofiti
Now it happened after these things that the Lord tested
Abraham with a tenth test. And he said to him, "Abraham."
Abraham answered in the language of the Temple, and he said
to him, "Here I am."

Like Onqelos, Neofiti translates the Hebrew word for "God"
with the Divine Name. But additionally, Neofiti adds that
this was Abraham's tenth test and that he spoke with God in
Hebrew.

Pseudo-Jonathan
Now it happened after these things, after Isaac and Ishmael
had quarreled, that Ishmael was saying, "It is fitting for me to
inherit my father because I am his firstborn son." Isaac was
saying, "It is fitting for me to inherit my father because I am
the son of Sarah, his wife, whereas you are the son of Hagar,
my mother's maidservant." Ishmael answered and said, "I am
more righteous than you are because I was circumcised at
thirteen years old, but if it had been my will to refuse, I would
not have handed over myself to be circumcised; but you were
circumcised at eight days old. If you had known, perhaps you
would not have given yourself over to be circumcised." Isaac
responded and said, "See, I am thirty-seven years old today,
and if the Holy One, blessed be He, would require all of my

members, I would not refuse." Immediately, these words were heard before the Lord of the World, and immediately, the Memra of the Lord tested Abraham and said to him, "Abraham," and he said to Him, "Here I am."

Pseudo-Jonathan literally translates the Hebrew text but inserts in the middle a detailed explanation of what is meant by the ambiguous phrase "after these things." This is not unlike the way in which Targum Song of Songs 1:1 uses the superlative phrase "The song of songs" as a springboard to draw comparison with other biblical songs and to teach about the Messiah.[28] Similarly, Pseudo-Jonathan explains what is meant by "these things" and uses the opportunity to convey a theological lesson.[29]

The Value of the Targums

From our discussion, it is evident that the Targums are interesting because of the Jewish traditions that they preserve, but we have not yet considered what value the Targums serve in helping to discover the Bible of Jesus' day. The first way in which the Targums contribute to our inquiry is that the biblical texts that make up the "Targum" Bible are all composed anonymously, which is empirical evidence from Jewish tradition that supports our earlier observation that anonymity was customary in the ancient world. Targum Onqelos, for instance, was attributed to Aquila, a second-century CE Jew who produced a Greek translation of the Hebrew Scriptures and other deuterocanonical texts (i.e., texts having a secondary canonical status).[30] Recent scholarship, however, generally rejects this

---

[28]   See pages 74-75.

[29]   Given the three different approaches to just this one verse, one may wonder if there is a common thread that runs through the Targums. According to Chilton and Flesher, there is: the philosophy of translation. They consider a "Targum" to be a very literal translation to which material is added seamlessly (ibid., 36), produced in accordance with seven basic rules (ibid., 39-54).

[30]   B. Megilla 3a.

attribution and considers Targum Onqelos to be written anonymously. Likewise, the Targum of the Prophets came to be known as "Targum Jonathan" because the Babylonian Talmud attributes it to Jonathan ben Uzziel, a first-century CE disciple of the famed Rabbi Hillel,[31] whose methods of biblical interpretation were known to the early Jesus movement. This, however, seems to be a late tradition, and it is best to regard the so-called Targum Jonathan as an anonymously and collaboratively composed work.[32] Pseudo-Jonathan and the Targums of the Ketuvim are likewise anonymous.

Second, scholarship has shown that the Targums of the Pentateuch grew over time, going through redactional stages before reaching their final forms. Neofiti drew upon Onqelos, and Pseudo-Jonathan drew from both of them. And this is to say nothing of other sources that may have contributed to their growth. These observations lend credence to what scholarship has supposed about the developmental process of the Hebrew Torah.

Third, the Targums' content and their methods of interpreting scripture shed light on the way in which the Scriptures were read in Jesus' day. Even though the Targums were written after the events of the New Testament, they, like the gospels, preserve traditions earlier than the Gospels themselves.[33] The broader genre of Targum is tied to Jewish worship of the Second Temple period in general, as we saw from Nehemiah 8, and to the synagogue in particular, as we discovered from the later talmudic evidence. Indeed, it has been suggested that the expansive nature of the Palestinian Targum is in part the result of the combination of a contextual translation, like we encounter in Onqelos, with the synagogue sermon.[34] By comparing Jesus' teaching on biblical texts with the Targums'

---

[31]   Ibid.

[32]   Harrington and Saldarini, *Targum Jonathan of the Former Prophets*, 1.

[33]   Chilton and Flesher, *The Targums*, 386.

[34]   McNamara, *Targum and Testament*, 82-83.

treatment of those texts, one finds in many cases that Jesus' teachings are not as innovative as some have thought. Some of Jesus' most profound explications of the Hebrew Scriptures—such as Leviticus 22:28 (see Luke 6:36) and Isaiah 6:9-10 (see Mark 4:11-12)[35]—may not be all that original. He may very well have been drawing from a shared interpretive tradition.

Ultimately, in the Targums one has access to copious data important for understanding the transmission of the Hebrew Bible, the history of Jewish exegesis, and the growth and development of the Aramaic language. Furthermore, it is an important chapter in the history of biblical interpretation. The Targums, however, are predated by the Greek translations of the Hebrew Scriptures, which are of even greater significance for our investigation. And it is to the Greek that we now turn our attention.

---

[35]   Chilton and Flesher, *The Targums*, 386-87.

8

THE BIBLE IN TRANSLATION, PART 2
THE SEPTUAGINT

> Once there were five elders who wrote the Torah in Greek for
> King Ptolemy, and that day was as hard for Israel as the day
> the golden calf was made, for the Torah could in no way be
> translated adequately.
>
> —b. Soferim 1.7

Of all the ancient translations of the Hebrew Bible, the ancient
Greek translations of the Hebrew Scriptures are inarguably the
most important for tracing the Hebrew Bible's literary history.
By comparing the ancient Greek manuscripts with the numerous
extant Hebrew manuscripts, including the biblical texts from
among the Dead Sea Scrolls as well as the later Tiberian
Masoretic manuscripts, we can see that the Septuagint's Hebrew
Vorlage differed significantly from the Masoretic Text. Some of
these differences were the result of scribal error or scribal
interpretation, while others resulted from a complex
transmission history that yielded different versions of the same
text.

The Old Greek translation of the Hebrew Scriptures is
commonly called the "Septuagint." But properly speaking, the
Septuagint (literally, "seventy" and therefore abbreviated with
the corresponding Roman numeral "LXX") is a third-century
BCE Greek translation of the *Torah* that was accomplished in
Alexandra, Egypt, for Greek-speaking Jews who were living
there. We know from the book of Jeremiah that ancestors of the
Jews relocated to Egypt in the sixth century BCE for fear of the
Babylonian king Nebuchadnezzar (Jeremiah 43:1-7), and
Aramaic texts from Elephantine, Egypt, demonstrate that Jewish

ancestors were still residing in Egypt in the fifth century BCE. In the latter half of the fourth century BCE, however, Alexander the Great conquered the Eastern Mediterranean world and began a program of Hellenization, which involved the promotion of Greek language and culture. As a result, by the third century BCE, Egyptian Jews had a need for a Greek translation of the Hebrew Scriptures.

Unfortunately, very little is known about the origins of the Septuagint. The earliest written tradition about the circumstances of the translation of the Torah into Greek comes from *The Letter of Aristeas*, a fictional letter probably dating to the latter half of the second century BCE,[1] which explains that the translation was produced at the request of the third-century King Ptolemy II (283–247 BCE) in Alexandria, Egypt. According to the letter, the Septuagint was not the first translation of the Hebrew Scriptures into Greek. Translations had already been produced but were executed carelessly (Aristeas, §30), for which reason a revision was needed.

According to Aristeas, Eliezer the Jewish High Priest, sent six elders from each of the twelve tribes of Israel, thus seventy-two in all, to Egypt with a Hebrew Torah (Aristeas, §46), in order to translate it into Greek for King Ptolemy so that it could then be added to the library of Alexandria.[2] Over the course of seventy-two days, the seventy-two translators produced the Septuagint, the Greek Torah (Aristeas, §307), and the translation was received with great favor:

> After the books had been read, the priests and the elders of the translators and the Jewish community and the leaders of the people stood up and said, that since so excellent and sacred and accurate a translation had been made, it was only right that it should remain as it was and no alteration should be

[1] Nickelsburg, *Jewish Literature between the Bible and the Mishnah: A Literary and Historical Introduction* (2d ed.), 198.
[2] The later rabbinic tractate *Soferim* (1.7-8) preserves a similar tradition.

made in it. And when the whole company expressed their approval, they bade them pronounce a curse in accordance with their custom upon any one who should make any alteration either by adding anything or changing in any way whatever any of the words which had been written or making any omission. This was a very wise precaution to ensure that the book might be preserved for all the future time unchanged (Aristeas, §§310-11).[3]

This, however, is a fictional account, which is, therefore, of minimal value to historians.[4]

It bears repeating that the Septuagint is the third century BCE translation of the *Torah* into Greek. The rest of the Hebrew Scriptures were translated by different individuals at different times. Nevertheless, scholars generally use the term "Septuagint" to refer to the Old Greek of the Pentateuch *and* the rest of the Jewish Bible, as well as a number of apocryphal works (see below). But in addition to the Septuagint, there were other Greek recensions (i.e., versions) and revisions that were produced over the course of the next few centuries.[5] This is significant for our investigation, in part, because it proves that there was not one official version of the Greek Old Testament in the first century CE, the time of Jesus and Paul. Perhaps the biggest reason why one authoritative version of the Old Testament could not have existed at that time is because no single scroll could contain the entire Bible. A Torah scroll itself

---

[3] Charles, ed., *Pseudepigrapha of the Old Testament*, 2.121. For a brief overview of *The Letter of Aristeas*, see Nickelsburg, *Jewish Literature between the Bible and the Mishnah* (2d ed.), 196-99.

[4] B. Megillah 9a preserves a tradition that supports the divine inspiration of the Septuagint. According to this story, King Ptolemy put seventy-two elders in different rooms to translate the Torah individually, and because of God's help, all seventy-two translations agreed on a number of critical issues.

[5] We have already mentioned Aquila's translation in chapter 7. For an overview of the Greek Old Testament, see Tov, *TCHB*[3], 127-47. For a discussion of the value of the Greek for textual criticism of the Hebrew Bible, see Tov, *The Text-Critical Use of the Septuagint in Biblical Research*.

is fairly unwieldy and not easy to use, so a scroll containing the entire Hebrew Bible would be of little practical value. To include all authoritative works together in one volume would have to wait until the codex (pl. "codices") came into use.

As we have noted previously, the codex was essentially the forerunner of today's bound book.[6] Like our modern book, it was made of numerous sheets that were stacked (not rolled), sewn together, and covered. Codices did not exist until the first century CE, which is why the Dead Sea Scrolls are not called the Dead Sea Codices. The codex did not come into common use until the third century, however, which is why a Bible could not have existed in the time of Jesus.[7]

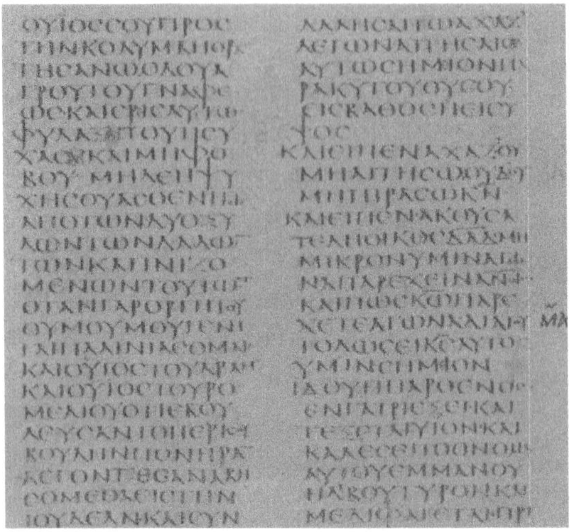

The two earliest codices of the entire Old Testament, Codex Vaticanus and Codex Sinaiticus (see figure 5), date to the early fourth century CE.[8] It is important to note that the Sinaiticus Bible includes not only the canonical Old and New Testaments but also a number of apocryphal works

Figure 5: An excerpt of Codex Sinaiticus (quire 43, folio 4, recto) containing portions of Isaiah 7. Image courtesy of the British Library.

and even certain works of the Common Era not included in the New Testament, such as the Shepherd of Hermas and the

---

6 See page 71.

7 See Roberts & Skeat, *The Birth of the Codex.*

8 Birdsall, "The Codex Sinaiticus: Its History and Significance," 33; Parker, *Codex Sinaiticus: The Story of the World's Oldest Bible,* 7.

Epistle of Barnabas. Codex Vaticanus contains a similar but not identical corpus.[9]

    This means, of course, that the oldest extant (i.e., still in existence) Christian Bible was not limited to the modern Protestant Canon.[10] In fact, when we examine a list of the New Testament's quotations and allusions to sacred Jewish texts, we see that the writers of the New Testament had a much bigger "Bible" than do twenty-first century Protestant Christians, as is clear from the references to Ascension of Isaiah, Assumption of Moses, Baruch, 1 Enoch, 1 Esdras, Judith, 1-4 Maccabees, Psalms of Solomon, Sirach, Susanna, Tobit, and Wisdom of Solomon.[11] The book of 1 Enoch, a work that is included only in the Bible of Ethiopian Christianity,[12] is alluded to and quoted multiple times in the New Testament. For example, Jude 6 refers to the fall of the angels mentioned in 1 Enoch and then in verses 14-15 quotes 1 Enoch 1:9:

> Now Enoch, the seventh from Adam, prophesied about these: "Behold, the Lord comes with ten-thousands of his holy ones to execute judgment on all and to convict all the ungodly of all their ungodly deeds that they have committed in such an ungodly way, and of all the harsh things that ungodly sinners have spoken against him."

We see, then, the early Septuagint codices are evidence of the Christian Bible's evolution long after the time of Jesus.

---

    [9] Both Sinaiticus and Vaticanus contain Tobit, Judith, 1-4 Maccabees, Wisdom of Solomon, and Sirach, but only Vaticanus contains Baruch and the Epistle of Jeremiah. For further discussion, see McDonald, *Formation of the Bible: The Story of the Church's Canon*, 77-86.

    [10] For further discussion, see Hengel, *The Septuagint as Christian Scripture: Its Prehistory and the Problem of Its Canon*, 57-74.

    [11] Aland, et al., eds., *The Greek New Testament* (4th revised ed.), 900-901.

    [12] See Nickelsburg, *1 Enoch 1: A Commentary on the Book of 1 Enoch, Chapters 1-36, 81-108*, 104-08.

The Septuagint and the Masoretic Text

Many words and phrases in the Septuagint reveal that the translators were working from a Hebrew *Vorlage* that differed from the Masoretic text that we use today, and therefore it is of great use in recovering earlier stages of the Hebrew Scriptures. Some differences are small. For instance, in Stephen's sermon, which includes a rehearsal of Israelite history, he notes that Jacob's family who had descended to Egypt numbered seventy-five (Acts 7:14). This agrees with the Septuagint's translation of Genesis 46:27 and Exodus 1:5. The Masoretic text, however, says in both cases that the number was only seventy, and this is the tradition that is preserved in all major English translations of the Old Testament.[13] This means that we should not be surprised when we encounter such contradictions elsewhere in the Bible.

In some cases, the Septuagint presents material not found in the Masoretic Text. At the beginning of their story, Cain and Abel present offerings to God, but only Abel's offering merits God's favor. Cain then becomes angry and is subsequently rebuked by God (Genesis 4:3-7). The story takes a turn in 4:8, where the Masoretic Text is most naturally translated as follows:

> And Cain said to Abel his brother, "..." Now it happened while they were in the field that Cain rose up against his brother Abel and killed him.

If this interpretation of the Hebrew is correct, then it would appear that whatever Cain said has been lost to us as a result of an early scribal omission, which is known as "haplography." On a rare occasion in the Hebrew Bible, the phrase "said to (someone)" can mean "spoke to (someone)." So we could translate "And Cain *spoke* to Abel his brother," which would not require a report of what Cain said. This is the solution adopted by many modern English translations, such as the KJV, ESV, NASB, and JPS. The NRSV, however, prefers the first option

---

[13]   E.g., ASV, ESV, KJV, NASB, NIV, and NRSV.

and follows "said to Abel his brother" with Cain's telling Abel to go out to the field with him. This translation is based on the Septuagint's version of Genesis 4:8:

> And Cain said to his brother Abel, "Let us go into the field." Now it happened while they were in the field that Cain rose up against his brother Abel and killed him.

This reading fills in what was lacking in the Masoretic Text tradition. It is difficult to determine which reading is to be preferred, however. On the one hand, the shorter and more difficult reading generally turns out to be the more original reading elsewhere. On the other hand, there are plenty of cases of haplography in the Hebrew Scriptures. I am of the opinion that the Septuagint preserves the original reading in this case, but it is possible that mine is not the correct explanation.[14]

In some cases, the Masoretic Text contains material that is absent from the Septuagint. According to the Masoretic text, Saul was only one year old when he became king and was still a toddler when he died (1 Samuel 13:1):

> Saul was one year old when he began to reign, and he reigned over Israel for two years.

Though it is not clear why, the Septuagint lacks this verse.

Elsewhere, the Septuagint lacks much longer texts. Its version of the David and Goliath story is almost half the length of the Masoretic text's version, the one with which most are familiar.[15] The Hebrew *Vorlage* of the Septuagint translation of Jeremiah is approximately one-sixth the size of the Masoretic text.[16]

---

[14] For further discussion and bibliography, see Jobes and Silva, *Invitation to the Septuagint* (2nd ed.), 239.

[15] Tov, *TCHB³*, 301.

[16] Ibid., 286-87. For additional examples, see 283-326.

Sometimes the reason for discrepancies between the Masoretic Text and the Septuagint are theologically motivated, as is the case with a textual variant in Deuteronomy 32:8. According to the Masoretic Text tradition, verses 8-9 can be translated:

When the Most-High apportioned the nations, when he divided the children of man, he established the boundaries of the nations, according to the number of the sons of Israel. For Yahweh's[17] portion is His people; Jacob is his allotted inheritance.

This tradition seems to suggest that "the Most-High" is part and parcel with Israel's God, who is presented as Lord over all. As we saw in chapter 1, however, the Septuagint and some of the Hebrew manuscripts of Deuteronomy discovered among the Dead Sea Scrolls feature variant, unorthodox readings, which contain "sons of God" as opposed to "sons of Israel." McCarthy observes that "sons of Israel" is a theological change added to the forerunner of the Masoretic Text to avoid the terribly uncomfortable reality that other manuscript traditions, including the Septuagint, bear witness; namely, that Deuteronomy 32 was not originally written from a monotheistic perspective.[18]

While the foregoing examples provide only a glimpse into the relationship of the Septuagint and the Masoretic Text, they are sufficient to demonstrate that the Hebrew Scriptures were still quite fluid in the late Second Temple period, the time of Jesus and the early Jesus movement.

---

[17] It has long been customary within Judaism to substitute God's personal name Yahweh with "the Lord" so as not to take "His name in vain." Gordis (*The Biblical Text in the Making: A Study of the Kethib-Qere*, 29-30) argues from biblical and extrabiblical evidence that this practice was well-stablished by the third century BCE. I break with that tradition here only because this particular textual issue requires us to be specific about the divine names.

[18] McCarthy, *Tiqquné Sopherim*, 211–14.

The Septuagint in the New Testament

From these examples, we can see that the Septuagint is a very different text tradition from the Masoretic Text,[19] which is why it is surprising to so many that the Septuagint was regarded by the writers of the New Testament as authoritative Scripture. The writers of the New Testament did not work from one fixed Hebrew text. Instead, they worked from Old Testament texts written in Hebrew, Aramaic, and Greek that differed in content from one another and that sometimes contradict one another. Whatever difficulties this causes for one's view of Scripture, this is the historical reality, and it cannot be ignored.

Because the Old Testament was written in Hebrew and Aramaic, one might expect early Christianity to have revered the "original" much as the Reformers did, but such was not the case. The Septuagint was for all intents and purposes *the* Bible for many Jews in antiquity. And since early Christianity was really no more than a movement within first-century Palestinian Judaism, it should be no surprise that the Septuagint was immensely important for the writers of the New Testament. In fact, those who regard Paul as the author of 2 Timothy must conclude that "all scripture," which the letter's author regards as "inspired[20] and profitable,"[21] includes both the Hebrew and the Greek, since Paul quotes extensively from the Septuagint in his writings.[22]

And because of this, certain Christian theological teachings were built upon Septuagintal tradition. We only need to go to the first chapter of the Gospel of Matthew to see this. After Joseph is informed by the angel of the Lord that Mary is

---

[19] For a thorough analysis of the Septuagintal and Masoretic versions of a biblical book, see Mackie, *Expanding Ezekiel.*

[20] Lit., "God-breathed."

[21] 2 Timothy 3:16-17.

[22] For instance, in a string of Old Testament quotations in Romans 3, Paul quotes from the Septuagint for at least four: Psalm 51:4 (Romans 3:4); Psalm 5:9 & 140:3 (Romans 3:13); Psalm 10:7 (Romans 3:14).

miraculously pregnant with Jesus, we are informed by the narrator:

> Now all of this transpired in order to fulfil what was spoken by the Lord through the prophet, "Behold, the virgin will conceive and will bear a son, and they will call his name, 'Immanuel,' which is translated, 'God is with us.'"

The prophecy quoted by Matthew is almost identical with the Septuagint's translation of Isaiah 7:14:

> Therefore, the Lord himself will give you a sign. Behold, the virgin will conceive and will bear a son, and you will call his name, "Immanuel."

According to the Septuagint, it is a woman who has not yet engaged in sexual intercourse – and is therefore unmarried – who will subsequently conceive the child. The Masoretic Text and the Great Isaiah Scroll from Qumran, on the other hand, present a very different reading:

> Therefore, the Lord himself will give you a sign. Behold, the young woman has conceived and will bear a son, and you will call his name, "Immanuel."

According to the Masoretic Text, it is a young woman of marriageable age—not a virgin—who has *already* conceived by the time the prophet Isaiah spoke these words to King Ahaz, almost eight hundred years before the birth of Jesus.

Let us turn our attention now to 1 Peter 2:6, whose quotation of two portions of Isaiah 28:16 resembles the Septuagint:

> For it stands in Scripture, "Behold, I lay in Zion a stone, a precious and chosen cornerstone. And whoever believes in him will not be put to shame."

The Hebrew text of this verse, however, is strikingly different from its rendering in the New Testament and in the Septuagint. According to the Masoretic text and manuscripts of Isaiah found among the Dead Sea Scrolls, the verse should be translated:

> Therefore, thus says the Lord GOD: Behold, I lay in Zion a stone, a tested stone, a precious corner of a sure foundation. Whoever believes will not be hasty.

There are two significant differences between the Masoretic Text's version of Isaiah 28:16 and the Greek rendering found in the Septuagint and in 1 Peter 2:6. First, according to 1 Peter, Scripture speaks of a stone that will yet be set. For this reason, it is understandable why a member of the early Jesus movement would read this passage as a prediction by Isaiah of something that came to be fulfilled in the person of Jesus. According to the Hebrew text, however, God's laying of the foundation stone has already been accomplished. It is not a prediction of something to come. The second difference concerns the last line of the verse. According to 1 Peter, the stone is a person, Jesus, and belief in him is what keeps one from reproach. In the Hebrew, however, the phrase "in him" is altogether absent, and the line indicates that the one who has true faith will not make hasty decisions that lead him to act against God's counsel spoken through the prophet. This is very similar to the situation recounted in Isaiah 7, where the prophet exhorts the king to patiently wait on God's intervention instead of responding to crisis rashly and imprudently.

Finally, we conclude our discussion by simply noting that Jesus' quotation of Isaiah 61:1-2 recorded in Jesus' synagogue sermon (Luke 4) belongs to the same text tradition as the Septuagint, not the Masoretic Text, which makes no mention of the recovery of sight to the blind. This on its own demonstrates that Jesus' "Bible" in Luke is distinct from the Masoretic Text.

***

In the course of our discussion of the Septuagint, we have learned that:

1. The Greek texts that came to be known as the Septuagint were translated from a Hebrew *Vorlage* or base text that differs significantly with the Masoretic Text.

2. The Septuagint was nevertheless authoritative Scripture for early Christianity.

3. Septuagintal renderings of Old Testament passages are the foundation of New Testament teachings, which makes the study of the Septuagint important for the study of Christian theology.

4. The earliest biblical codices include many religious texts not included in the Jewish Bible and the Protestant Old Testament.

5. The "Bible" of Jesus and the writers of the New Testament was very different from the Jewish Bible/Old Testament that is read today in the West.

Taken together, this information radically affects the way we think about the Bible and the history of its transmission.

CONCLUSION

Over the course of our investigation, we have learned that in Jesus' time, the canon of the Hebrew Bible was not yet established. The broader community of faith had yet to collectively determine once and for all which texts would make the cut and which would not. But not only was the canon of the Hebrew Bible yet to be settled, many of the texts that would eventually comprise the Hebrew Bible were themselves still textually fluid. The text tradition that would serve as the basis for the Tiberian Masoretic Bible was largely fixed at that point, but it was not completely crystallized down to the very letter until much later. That would have to wait until the last few centuries of the Common Era. So, the Hebrew Bible/Old Testament did not yet exist in Jesus' day. Until the fourth century CE, when the first biblical codices were produced, Christianity functioned with Scriptures but without a Bible.

Some readers may still find this difficult to fathom, especially those in whose religious traditions a theology of Scripture takes center stage. This is understandable given that few religious congregations devote much time to the exploration of the Hebrew Bible's history. And while it is not the purpose of this book to engage in theological inquiry, much less to settle theological debates, what we have learned about the history of the Hebrew Bible and its meaning for its *ancient* audiences will hopefully help to foster inquiry and dialogue about the Hebrew Bible's origins among those for whom theology is important. Scholarship is, after all, an ongoing dialogue. And if for you, the reader, this book serves as an entry into this dialogue, I consider it a success.

BIBLIOGRAPHY

Abegg Jr., Martin G., Peter Flint, and Eugene Ulrich. *The Dead Sea Scrolls Bible: The Oldest Known Bible Translated for the First Time into English.* San Francisco: HarperOne, 2012.

Adrados, Francisco Rodríguez. *A History of the Greek Language from Its Origins to the Present.* Translated by Francisca Rojas del Canto. Leiden: Brill, 2005.

Aḥituv, Shmuel. *Echoes from the Past: Hebrew and Cognate Inscriptions from the Biblical Period.* Jerusalem: Carta, 2009.

Aland, Barbara, et al., eds., *The Greek New Testament* 4th rev. ed. New York: American Bible Society, 2001.

Algaze, Guillermo. *The Uruk World System: The Dynamics of Expansion of Early Mesopotamian Civilization.* 2nd ed. Chicago: University of Chicago Press, 2005.

Baines, John. *Visual and Written Culture in Ancient Egypt.* Oxford: Oxford University Press, 2007.

Bard, Kathryn A. *An Introduction to the Archaeology of Ancient Egypt.* 2nd. ed. New York: Wiley & Sons, 2015.

Barthélemy, Dominique. *Studies in the Text of the Old Testament: An Introduction to the Hebrew Old Testament Text Project.* English Translation of the Introductions to Volumes 1, 2, and 3 *Critique Textuelle de l'Ancien Testement.* Winona Lake, IN: Eisenbrauns, 2012.

Barton, John. "Postexilic Hebrew Prophecy." Pages 489-94 in *The Anchor Bible Dictionary.* Vol. 5. Edited by David Noel Freedman. New York: Doubleday, 1992.

———. *Reading the Old Testament: Method in Biblical Study.* London: Darton, Longman & Todd, 1996.

———. *The Theology of the Book of Amos.* Old Testament Theology. New York: Cambridge University Press, 2012.

Beit-Arié, M., C. Sirat, and M. Glatzer. *Codices Hebraicis Litteris Exarati Quo Tempore Scripti Fuerint Exhibentes.* Vol. 1. of *Monumenta Palaeographica Medii Aevi,* Series Hebraica. Turnhout: Brepols, 1997.

Ben Asher, Elijah, and Christian D. Ginsburg. *The Massoreth ha-Massoreth of Elias Levita, Being an Exposition of the Massoretic Notes on the Hebrew Bible.* London: Longmans, Green, Reader, and Dyer, 1867.

Birdsall, J. "The Codex Vaticanus: Its History and Significance." Pages 33-41 in *The Bible as Book: The Transmission of the Greek Text.* Edited by Scot McKendrick & Oralaith A. O'Sullivan. London: British Library, 2003.

Black, Jeremy, et al. *The Literature of Ancient Sumer.* Oxford: Oxford University Press, 2004.

Black, Matthew. *An Aramaic Approach to the Gospels and the Acts.* 3rd ed. London: Oxford University Press, 1967.

Blau, Joshua. *Phonology and Morphology of Biblical Hebrew.* Winona Lake, IN: Eisenbrauns, 2010.

Blenkinsopp, Joseph. *A History of Prophecy in Israel.* Rev. and enl. ed. Louisville: Westminster John Knox, 1996.

———. *Isaiah 1-39.* Anchor Bible 19. New York: Doubleday, 2000.

Bottéro, Jean, Clarisse Herrenschmidt, and Jean-Pierre Vernant. *Ancestors of the West: Writing, Reasoning, and Religion in Mesopotamia, Elam, and Greece.* Translated by Teresa Lavender Fagan. Chicago: Chicago University Press, 2000.

Boyce, Mary. *Textual Studies for the Study of Zoroastrianism.* Chicago: University of Chicago Press, 1984.

Brettler, Marc Z. *The Creation of Ancient Israel.* New York: Routledge, 1995.

Breuer, Mordechai. *The Biblical Text in the Jerusalem Crown Edition and Its Sources in the Masora and Manuscripts.* Jerusalem: Keren Ha-Masora, 2003. (Heb.)

Brogan, John J. "Can I Have Your Autograph? Uses and Abuses of Textual Criticism in Formulating an Evangelical Doctrine of Scripture." Pages 93-111 in *Evangelicals and Scripture: Tradition, Authority, and Hermeneutics.* Edited by Vincent Bacote, Laura C. Miguélez, and Dennis L. Oklholm. Downers Grove, IL: IVP, 2004.

Buth, Randall, and R. Steven Notley, eds. *The Language Environment of First Century Judaea: Jerusalem Studies in the Synoptic Gospels.* Jewish and Christian Perspectives 2. Leiden: Brill, 2014.

Callender, Gae. "The Middle Kingdom." Pages 148-83 in *The Oxford History of Ancient Egypt.* Edited by Ian Shaw. Oxford: Oxford University Press, 2000.

Calvin, John. *Commentaries on the Book of Joshua.* Translated by Henry Beveridge. Grand Rapids, MI: Eerdmans, 1949.

Carr, David M. *Writing on the Tablets of the Heart: Origins of Scripture and Literature.* Oxford: Oxford University Press, 2005.

———. "The Tel Zayit Abecedary in (Social) Context." Pages 113-30 in *Literate Culture and Tenth-Century Canaan: The Tel Zayit Abecedary in Context.* Edited by Ron E. Tappy and P. Kyle McCarter. Winona Lake, IN: Eisenbrauns, 2008.

Carson, D. A., and Douglas J. Moo. *An Introduction to the New Testament.* 2nd ed. Grand Rapids, MI: Zondervan, 2008.

Casey, Maurice. *An Aramaic Approach to Q: Sources for the Gospels of Matthew and Luke.* New York: Cambridge University Press, 2002.

Charles, Robert Henry, ed. *Pseudepigrapha of the Old Testament.* 2 vols. Oxford: Clarendon Press, 1913.

Charlesworth, James H. "Pseudepigrapha, OT." Pages 537–540 in *The Anchor Bible Dictionary.* Vol. 5. Edited by David Noel Freedman. New York: Doubleday, 1992.

Cohen, Abraham, ed. *The Minor Tractates of the Talmud. Translated into English with Notes, Glossary and Indices.* 2 vol. Soncino Press: London, 1965.

Cohen, Maimon. *The Kethib and Qeri System in the Biblical Text: A Linguistic Analysis of the Various Traditions Based on the Manuscript in "Keter Aram Tsova."* Jerusalem: The Hebrew University Magnes Press, 2007.

Cohen, Menachem, ed. *Mikra'ot Gedolot 'Haketer.'* Ramat Gan: Bar Ilan University Press, 1992-.

Cohen, Shaye. *From the Maccabees to the Mishnah.* 2d ed. Louisville, KY: Westminster John Knox, 2006.

Davies, Philip R. *In Search of "Ancient Israel:" A Study in Biblical Origins.* The Library of Hebrew Bible/Old Testament Studies. Bloomsbury T&T Clark: New York, 1992.

Deijl, Aarnoud van der. *Protest or Propaganda: War in the Old Testament Book of Kings and in Contemporaneous Ancient Near Eastern Texts.* Studia Semitica Neerlandica 51 Leiden: Brill, 2008.

Dershowitz, Idan. "The Secret History of Leviticus" New York Times. Op. ed. 7/21/2018. https://www.nytimes.com/2018/07/21/opinion/sunday/bible-prohibit-gay-sex.html.

Dever, William G. *What Did the Biblical Writers Know and When Did They Know It? What Archaeology Can Tell Us about the Reality of Ancient Israel.* Grand Rapids, MI: Eerdmans, 2001.

Donner, H., and W. Röllig, *Kanaanäische und Aramäische Inschriften.* 3 vols. Wiesbaden: Otto Harrassowitz, 1964.

Dost, Christopher. *The Sub-Loco Notes in the Former Prophets of Biblia Hebraica Stuttgartensia.* Texts & Studies 12. Piscataway, NJ: Gorgias, 2016.

———. "Esther 1." In the *Targum Bible.* Edited by Paul Flesher. Waco, TX: Baylor University Press, Forthcoming 2019.

————. "Song of Songs." In the *Targum Bible*. Edited by Paul Flesher. Waco, TX: Baylor University Press, Forthcoming 2019.

Dotan, Aron. "The Beginnings of Masoretic Vowel Notation." Pages 21-33 in *1972 and 1973 Proceedings of the First Congress of the IOMS*. Edited by H. M. Orlinksy. Missoula: Scholars Press, 1974.

————. *The Awakening of Word Lore: From the Masora to the Beginnings of Hebrew Lexicography*. The Academy of the Hebrew Language Sources and Studies VII; Jerusalem: The Academy of the Hebrew Language, 2005.

————. "Masorah." Pages 603-56 in vol. 13 of *Encyclopaedia Judaica*. 2d ed. Edited by Michael Berenbaum and Fred Skolnik. Detroit: Macmillan Reference USA, 2007.

Dotan, Aron and Nurit Reich, eds. *A Complete Alphabetic Collection of Comments from the Masora in the Leningrad Codex*. Accordance Bible Software, 2014.

Ehrman, Bart D. *Jesus, Interrupted: Revealing the Hidden Contradictions in the Bible (and Why We Don't Known about Them)*. New York: HarperOne, 2009.

————. *Forged: Writing in the Name of God—Why the Bible's Authors Are Not Who We Think They Are*. New York: HarperOne, 2011.

————. *A Brief Introduction of the New Testament*. 3rd ed. Oxford: Oxford University Press, 2013.

Elbogen, Ismar. *Jewish Liturgy: A Comprehensive History*. Translated by Raymond P. Scheindlin. Philadelphia/New York: The Jewish Publication Society/The Jewish Theological Seminary of America, 1993.

Englund, Robert K. "Accounting in Proto-Cuneiform." Pages 32-50 in *The Oxford Handbook of Cuneiform Culture*. Edited by Karen Radner and Eleanor Robson. Oxford: Oxford University Press, 2011.

Eusebius. *Ecclesiastical History and the Martyrs of Palestine.* Translated with introduction and notes by Hugh Jackson Lawlor and John Ernest Leonard Oulton. Vol. 1. New York: MacMillan, 1927.

Finkelstein, Israel, and Amihai Mazar: *The Quest for the Historical Israel: Debating Archaeology and the History of Early Israel.* Edited by Brian B. Schmidt. Atlanta: Society of Biblical Literature, 2007.

Fitzmyer, Joseph A. *The Semitic Background to the New Testament.* Grand Rapids, MI: Eerdmans, 1997.

Fitzmyer, Joseph A., and Daniel J. Harrington. *A Manual of Palestinian Aramaic Texts.* Biblica et Orienta 34. Rome: Biblical Institute, 1978.

Fleming, Daniel E. *The Legacy of Judah's Bible: History, Politics, and the Reinscribing of the Tradition.* New York: Cambridge University Press, 2012.

Flesher, Paul V. M., and Bruce D. Chilton. *The Targums: A Critical Introduction.* Waco, TX: Baylor, 2011.

Flusser, David, with R. Steven Notley. *The Sage of Galilee: Rediscovering Jesus' Genius.* Introduction by James H. Charlesworth. Grand Rapids, MI: Eerdmans, 2007.

Foster, Benjamin R. "Transmission of Knowledge," Pages 245-52 in *A Companion to the Ancient Near East.* Edited by Daniel C. Snell. Blackwell Companions to the Ancient World. Oxford: Blackwell, 2005.

―――. *Before the Muses: An Anthology of Akkadian Literature.* 3rd ed. Bethesda, MD: CDL Press, 2005.

Foster, Benjamin R., and Karen Polinger Foster. *Civilizations of Ancient Iraq.* Princeton: Princeton University Press, 2009.

Frahm, Eckart. "Keeping Company with Men of Learning: The King as Scholar." Pages 508-32 in *The Oxford Handbook of Cuneiform Culture.* Edited by Karen Radner and Eleanor Robson. Oxford: Oxford University Press, 2011.

Freedman, David Noel, Astrid B. Beck, Bruce E. Zuckerman, Marilyn J. Lundberg, & James A. Sanders, eds. *The Leningrad Codex: A Facsimile Edition*. Grand Rapids, MI: Eerdmans, 1998.

Freedman, H., trans. *Genesis 1*. Vol. 1 of *Midrash Rabbah*. Edited by H. Freedman and Maurice Simon. New York: Soncino, 1983.

Friedman, Richard Elliott. "Torah (Pentateuch)." Pages 605– 622 in *The Anchor Bible Dictionary*. Vol. 6. Edited by David Noel Freedman. New York: Doubleday, 1992.

Friedman, Matti. *The Aleppo Codex: A True Story of Obsession, Faith, and the Pursuit of an Ancient Bible*. New York: Algonquin Books, 2012.

García Martínez, Florentino & Eibert J.C. Tigchelaar. *The Dead Sea Scrolls Study Edition*. 2 vols. New York: Brill, 1997-1998.

Garfinkel, Stephen. "Applied *Peshat*: Historical-Critical Method and Religious Meaning." *Journal of the Ancient Near Eastern Society* 22.1 (1993): 19-28.

Gaster, T. H., "Psalm 29." *Jewish Quarterly Review* 37 (1946-1947): 55-65.

Geisler, Norman L. *Inerrancy*. Grand Rapids, MI: Zondervan, 1980.

Geller, Stephen A. "Wellhausen and Kaufmann." Midstream (December, 1985): 39-48.

Gianto, Agustinus. "Archaic Biblical Hebrew." Pages 19-30 in *A Handbook of Biblical Hebrew: Volume 1: Periods, Corpora, and Reading Traditions*. Edited by W. Randall Garr and Steven E. Fassberg. Winona Lake, IN: Eisenbrauns, 2016.

Ginsberg, H. L. "Reflexes of Sargon in Isaiah after 715 B.C.E." *Journal of the American Oriental Society* 88.1 (1968): 47-53.

Ginsburg, Christian D. *The Massorah: Compiled from Manuscripts. Alphabetically and Lexically Arranged.* 4 vols. London, 1880–1905. Repr., New York: KTAV, 1975.

―――. *Introduction to the Massoretico-Critical Edition of the Hebrew Bible.* London: Trinitarian Bible Society, 1897. Reprinted with prolegomenon by Harry M. Orlinsky; New York: KTAV, 1966.

Glassman, Gary, producer. *The Bible's Buried Secrets.* Providence Pictures, produced for Nova in association with National Geographic Channel and WGBH Educational Foundation. 2009.

Glassner, Jean-Jeaques. *Mesopotamian Chronicles.* Writings from the Ancient World 19. Atlanta: Society of Biblical Literature, 2004.

Gordis, Robert. *The Biblical Text in the Making: A Study of the Kethib-Qere.* Aug. with prolegomenon. New York: KTAV, 1971.

Goshen-Gottstein, Moshe. "The Authenticity of the Aleppo Codex." *Textus* 1 (1960): 17-58.

―――, ed. *The Aleppo Codex, Volume 1, The Plates.* Jerusalem: Magnes, 1976.

Hallo, William W., and K. Lawson Younger. *The Context of Scripture.* 4 vols. New York: Brill, 1997-2017.

Hanson, P. D. "Apocalypticism." Pages 28-34 in *Interpreters Dictionary of the Bible: Supplement.* Nashville: Abingdon, 1976.

Hengel, Martin. *The Septuagint as Christian Scripture: Its Prehistory and the Problem of Its Canon.* Introduction by Robert Hanhart. Translated by Mark E. Biddle. New York: T & T Clark, 2002.

Hoffmeier, James K. *Israel in Egypt: Evidence for the Authenticity of the Exodus Tradition.* Oxford: Oxford University Press, 1996.

Hornkohl "Transitional Biblical Hebrew." Pages 31-42 in *A Handbook of Biblical Hebrew: Volume 1: Periods, Corpora, and Reading Traditions.* Edited by W. Randall Garr and Steven E. Fassberg. Winona Lake, IN: Eisenbrauns, 2016.

Jacobsen, Thorkild. *The Treasures of Darkness: A History of Mesopotamian Religion.* New Haven, CT: Yale University Press, 1976.

Jeremias, Jörg. *The Book of Amos.* Old Testament Library. Louisville, KY: Westminster John Knox Press, 1998.

Jobes, Karen, and Moíses Silva. *Invitation to the Septuagint.* 2nd ed. Grand Rapids, MI: Baker, 2015.

Kaiser, Jr., Walter C. *The Old Testament Documents: Are They Reliable and Relevant?* Downers Grove, IL: InterVarsity Press, 2001.

Kaufman, Stephen A. "The Job Targum from Qumran." *Journal of the American Oriental Society* 93.3 (1973): 317-27.

Kelley, Page H., Daniel S. Mynatt, and Timothy G. Crawford. *The Masorah of Biblia Hebraica Stuttgartensia: Introduction and Annotated Glossary.* Grand Rapids, MI: Eerdmans, 1998.

Kahle, Paul E. *The Cairo Geniza.* 2nd ed. New York: Praeger, 1959.

Khan, Geoffrey. *A Short Introduction to the Tiberian Masoretic Bible and its Reading Tradition.* 2nd ed. Gorgias Handbooks 25. Piscataway, NJ: Gorgias, 2013.

Kitchen, K. A. *On the Reliability of the Old Testament.* Grand Rapids, MI: Eerdmans, 2003.

Kraus, Hans-Joachim. *Psalms 1-59.* A Continental Commentary. Translated by Hilton C. Oswald. Minneapolis: Fortress, 1993.

———. *Psalms 60-150.* A Continental Commentary. Translated by Hilton C. Oswald. Minneapolis: Fortress, 1993.

Krüger, Thomas. *Qoheleth: A Commentary.* Hermeneia. Edited by O. C. Dean, Jr.. Edited by Klaus Baltzer. Minneapolis: Fortress, 2004.

Kugel, James L. *The Bible as It Was*. Cambridge, MA: Belknap, 1997.

Kuhrt, Amélie. *The Ancient Near East c. 3000-330 BC*. 2 vols. New York: Routledge, 1995.

Kutscher, Eduard Yechezkel. *A History of the Hebrew Language*. Edited by Raphael Kutscher. Jerusalem: Magness, 1982.

Lam, Joseph, and Dennis Pardee, "Standard/Classical Biblical Hebrew." Pages 1-18 in *A Handbook of Biblical Hebrew: Volume 1: Periods, Corpora, and Reading Traditions*. Edited by W. Randall Garr and Steven E. Fassberg. Winona Lake, IN: Eisenbrauns, 2016.

Law, Timothy Michael. *When God Spoke Greek: The Septuagint and the Making of the Christian Bible*. Oxford: Oxford University Press, 2013.

Lawson Younger, Jr., K. *Ancient Conquest Accounts: A Study in Ancient Near Eastern and Biblical History Writing*. Journal for the Study of the Old Testament Supplemental Series 98; Sheffield: Sheffield Academic Press, 1990.

Leith, May Joan Winn. "Israel among the Nations: The Persian Period." Pages 276-316 in *The Oxford History of the Biblical World*. Edited by Michael D. Coogan. Oxford, 1998.

Levine, Amy-Jill, and Marc Zvi Brettler, eds. *The Jewish Annotated New Testament*. Oxford: Oxford University Press, 2011.

Lightfoot, John. *A Commentary on the New Testament from the Talmud and Hebraica*. 4 vols. With introduction by R. Laird Harris. Grand Rapids, MI: Baker, 1979. Repr. of *A Commentary on the New Testament from the Talmud and Hebraica*. 4 vols. Oxford: Oxford University Press, 1859.

Limburg, James. "Psalms, Book of." Pages 522-36 in *The Anchor Bible Dictionary*. Vol. 5. Edited by David Noel Freedman. New York: Doubleday, 1992.

Lindenberger, James M. *Ancient Aramaic and Hebrew Letters.* Writings from the Ancient World 4. Edited by Kent Harold Richards. Atlanta: Scholars Press, 1994.

Loewinger, D. S. *Codex Cairo of the Bible from the Karaite Synagogue At Abbasiya.* Jerusalem: Makor Press, 1971.

Longenecker, Richard. *Biblical Exegesis in the Apostolic Period.* 2nd ed. Grand Rapids, MI: Eerdmans, 1999.

MacDonald, M.C.A. "Literacy in an Oral Environment." Pages 49-118 in *Writing and Ancient Near Eastern Society: Papers in Honour of Alan R. Millard.* Edited by Piotr Bienkowski, Christopher Mee, and Elizabeth Slater. Library of Hebrew Bible/Old Testament Studies 426. New York: T & T Clark, 2005.

Mahoney, Timothy P., producer. *Patterns of Evidence: The Exodus.* Thinking Man Films, 2015.

Marcos, Natalio Fernández. *The Septuagint in Context: Introduction to the Greek Version of the Bible.* Translated by Wilfred G. E. Watson. Leiden: Brill, 2000.

Marcus, David. *Scribal Wit: Aramaic Mnemonics in the Leningrad Codex.* Texts & Studies 10. Piscataway, NJ: Gorgias, 2013.

Marcus, David and James A. Sanders, "What's Critical about a Critical Edition of the Bible?" *Biblical Archeology Review* 39:6 (2013): 60-65.

Mark, Samuel. *From Egypt to Mestopotamia: A Study in Predynastic Trade Routes.* Studies in Nautical Archaeology 4. College Station: Texas A&M, 1997.

Martín Contreras, Elvira. "Masora and Masoretic Interpretation." Pages 542-550 in vol. 1 of *The Oxford Encyclopedia of Biblical Interpretation.* Edited by Steven L. McKenzie. Oxford: Oxford University Press, 2013.

———. "Medieval Masoretic Text." Pages 420-29 in vol. 1a of *Textual History of the Bible.* Edited by Armin Lange and Emmanuel Tov. Leiden: Brill, 2016.

————. "Ketib/Qere." Pages 145-47 in vol. 15 in *Encyclopedia of the Bible and its Reception*. Edited by Christine Helmer et al. Berlin: De Gruyter, 2017.

Martín Contreras, Elvira, and Lorena Miralles Macia. *From the Rabbis to the Masoretes*. Journal of Ancient Judaism Supplements 13. Göttingen: Vandenhoeck et Ruprecht, 2014.

McCarthy, Carmel. *The Tiqqune Sopherim and Other Theological Corrections in the Masoretic Text of the Old Testament*. Freiburg & Göttingen: Universitätsverlag, 1981.

McDonald, Lee Martin. "Wherein Lies Authority? A Discussion of Books, Texts, and Translations." Pages 203-40 in *Exploring the Origins of the Bible: Canon Formation in Historical, Literary, and Theological Perspective*. Edited by Craig A. Evans and Emanuel Tov. Grand Rapids, MI: Baker, 2008.

————. *Formation of the Bible: The Story of the Church's Canon*. Peabody, MA: Hendrickson, 2012.

McDonald, Lee Martin, and Stanley E. Porter. *Early Christianity and Its Sacred Literature*. Peabody, MA: Hendrickson, 2000.

McDowell, Josh, and Sean McDowell. *The New Evidence that Demands a Verdict: Life-Changing Truth for a Skeptical World*. Nashville: Thomas Nelson Publishers, 2017.

McNamara, Martin. *Targum and Testament Revisited: Aramaic Paraphrases of the Hebrew Bible*. 2nd ed. Grand Rapids, MI: Eerdmans, 2010.

Milik, J. T. "Notes by Menaḥem M. Kasher on the Fragments of Targum to Leviticus and the Commentary." Pages 92-93 in Vol. 6 of *Discoveries of the Judean Desert*. Edited by Roland de Vaux and J. T. Milik. Oxford: Clarendon Press, 1977

Millard, Alan. "The Ostracon from the Days of David found at Khirbet Qeiyafa." *Tyndale Bulletin* 62.1 (2011): 1-13.

Miller, Jeff. Review of *God's Word Alone*, by Matthew Barrett. *Stone-Campbell Journal* 20 (Fall 2017): 257-59.

Morgenstern, Matthew. "Late Biblical Hebrew." Pages 43-54 in *A Handbook of Biblical Hebrew: Volume 1: Periods, Corpora, and Reading Traditions.* Edited by W. Randall Garr and Steven E. Fassberg. Winona Lake, IN: Eisenbrauns, 2016.

Muraoka, "The Aramaic of the Old Targum of Job from Qumran Cave XI." *Journal of Jewish Studies* 25 (1974): 425-43.

Neusner, Jacob, ed. *The Babylonian Talmud: A Translation and Commentary.* Peabody, MA: Hendrickson, 2010.

———. *The Jerusalem Talmud: A Translation and Commentary.* Peabody, MA: Hendrickson, 2010.

Nevalainen, Terttu. *An Introduction to Early Modern English.* Edinburgh: Edinburgh University Press, 2006.

Nickelsburg, George W. E. *1 Enoch 1: A Commentary on the Book of 1 Enoch, Chapters 1-36, 81-108.* Edited by Klaus Baltzer. Minneapolis: Fortress, 2001.

———. *Jewish Literature between the Bible and the Mishnah: A Literary and Historical Introduction.* 2nd ed. Minneapolis: Fortress, 2005.

Nissen, Hans J. *The Early History of the Ancient Near East: 9000-2000 B.C.* Chicago, 1988. Translated by Elizabeth Lutzeier, with Kenneth J. Northcott. *Grundzüge einer Geschichte der Frühzeit des Vorderen Orients.* Darmstadt: Wissenschaftliche Buchgesellschaft, 1983.

Níssínen, Martí, ed. *Prophecy in Its Ancient Near Eastern Context: Mesopotamian, Biblical, and Arabian Perspectives.* SBL Symposium Series 13. Atlanta: Society of Biblical Literature, 2000.

———. *Prophets and Prophecy in the Ancient Near East.* With contributions by C. L. Seow and Robert K. Ritner. Writings from the Ancient World 12. Atlanta: Society of Biblical Literature, 2003.

Noegel, Scott B., and Gary A. Rendsburg, *Solomon's Vineyard: Literary and Linguistic Studies in the Song of Solomon*. Leiden: Brill, 2009.

Ofer, Yosef. "The History and Authority of the Aleppo Codex." Pages 25-50 in *Jerusalem Crown: Companion Volume*. Edited by Mordechai Glatzer. Jerusalem: Ben-Zvi, 2002.

Parker, D. C. *Codex Sinaiticus: The Story of the World's Oldest Bible*. London: British Museum, 2010.

Patel, Vimal. "What Neil deGrasse Tyson Thinks Higher Ed Gets Wrong." *The Chronicles of Higher Education* 65.3 (September 16, 2018): A6.

Person Jr., Raymond F. *The Deuteronomic History and the Book of Chronicles: Scribal Works in an Oral World*. Ancient Israel and Its Literature. Atlanta: Society of Biblical Literature, 2010.

Petersen, David L. "Eschatology: Old Testament." Pages 575-79 in *The Anchor Bible Dictionary*. Vol.2. Edited by David Noel Freedman. New York: Doubleday, 1992.

Polachek, I., I. F. Salkin, D. Schenhav, & Ofer, M. Maggen, and J. H. Haines. "Damage to an Ancient Parchment Document by Aspergillus." *Mycopathologia* 106 (1989): 89–93.

Porter, Stanley. "Language and Translation of the New Testament." Pages --- in *The Oxford Handbook of Biblical Studies*. Oxford Handbooks. Edited by J. W. Rogerson and Judith M. Lieu. Oxford: Oxford University Press, 2008.

Pritchard, James B., ed. *Ancient Near Eastern Texts Relating to the Old Testament*. 3rd ed. with Supplement. Princeton: Princeton University Press, 1969.

Radner, Karen, and Eleanor Robson, eds. *The Oxford Handbook of Cuneiform Culture*. Oxford: Oxford University Press, 2011.

Ragobert, Thierry, Director. *The Bible Unearthed: The Making of a Religion*. Episode 4. Brooklyn, NY: Icarus Films, 2005.

Renz, Johannes, and Wolfgang Röllig. *Handbuch der Althebräischen Epigraphik. Die Althebräischen Inschriften.* 3 vols. Darmstadt: Wissenschaftliche Buchgesellschaft, 1995-2003.

Richards, Suzanne, ed. *Near Eastern Archaeology: A Reader.* Winona Lake, IN: Eisenbrauns, 2003.

Richelle, Matthieu. *The Bible and Archaeology.* Forward by Alan B. Millard. Peabody, MA: Hendrickson, 2018.

Roaf, Michael. *Cultural Atlas of Mesopotamia and the Ancient Near East.* Oxford: Andromeda Oxford, 1990.

Roberts, C. H., and T. C. Skeat, *The Birth of the Codex.* London: The British Academy, 1983. Reprint Oxford University Press, 2004.

Rollston, Christoph A. "The Phoenician Script of the Tel Zayit Abecedary and Putative Evidence for Israelite Literacy." Pages 61-96 in *Literate Culture and Tenth-Century Canaan: The Tel Zayit Abecedary in Context.* Ron E. Tappy and P. Kyle McCarter. Winona Lake, IN: Eisenbrauns, 2008.

―――. *Writing and Literacy in the World of Ancient Israel: Epigraphic Evidence from the Iron Age.* Archaeology and Biblical Studies 11. Atlanta: Society of Biblical Literature, 2010.

Rubin, Aaron D. *A Brief Introduction to the Semitic Languages.* Gorgias Handbooks 19. Piscataway, NJ: Gorgias, 2010.

Rubio, Gonzalo. "The Languages of the Ancient Near East." Pages 79-109 in *A Companion to the Ancient Near East.* Edited by Daniel C. Snell. Blackwell Companions to the Ancient World. Oxford: Blackwell, 2005.

Sailhamer, John H. *The Meaning of the Pentateuch: Revision, Revelation, and Interpretation.* Downers Grove, IL: IVP Academic, 2009.

Satlow, Michael L. *Creating Judaism: History, Tradition, Practice.* Columbia University, 2006.

Schiffman, Lawrence H. *Qumran and Jerusalem: Studies in the Dead Sea Scrolls and the History of Judaism.* Eerdmans. 2010.

Schmid, Konrad. English: *The Old Testament: A Literary History.* Translated by Linda M. Maloney. Minneapolis: Fortress Press, 2012.

Schniedewind, William M. *A Social History of Hebrew: Its Origins Through the Rabbinic Period.* New Haven: Yale University Press, 2013.

Seow, Choon-Leong. *Ecclesiastes: A New Translation with Introduction and Commentary.* The Anchor Bible 18C. New York: Doubleday, 1997.

Simon, Uriel. "Jewish Exegesis in Spain and Provence, and in the East, in the Twelfth and Thirteenth Centuries." Pages 372-87 in Magne Sæbø, *Hebrew Bible/Old Testament: The History of Its Interpretation. Volume II: From the Renaissance to the Enlightenment.* Göttingen: Vandenhoeck & Ruprecht, 2008.

Ska, Jean-Louis. *Introduction to Reading the Pentateuch.* Winona Lake, IN: Eisenbrauns, 2006.

Smith, Huston. *The Illustrated World's Religions: A Guide to Our Wisdom Traditions.* New York: HarperCollins 1995.

Smith, Mark S. *The Origins of Biblical Monotheism.* New York: Oxford University Press, 2001.

———. *The Priestly Vision of Genesis 1.* Minneapolis: Fortress, 2010.

Sommer, Benjamin. *A Prophet Reads Scripture: Allusion in Isaiah 40-66.* Contraversions: Jews and Other Differences. Stanford: Stanford University Press, 1998.

Sparks, Kenton L. *Ancient Texts for the Study of the Hebrew Bible: A Guide to the Background Literature.* Peabody, MA: Hendrickson, 2005.

Spinoza, Benedict of. *A Theological-Political Treatise.* Part II. Translated by R. H. M. Elwes. Published in *The Chief Works of Benedict de Spinoza, Translated from the Latin, with an Introduction* by R. H. M. Elwes. Vol. 1: Introduction, Tractatus Theologico-Politicus, Tractatus Politicus, Revised Ed. London, Bell and Sons, 1891.

Sternberg, Meir. *The Poetics of Biblical Narrative: Ideological Literature and the Drama of Reading.* Bloomington: Indiana University Press, 1985.

Strack, Hermann L., and Paul Billerbeck, *Kommentar zum neuen Testament aus Talmud und Midrash.* Vol. 1 of *Das Evangelium nach Matthäus Erläutert aus Talmud und Midrasch.* 7th ed. Munich: Beck, 1978.

Stuckenbruck, Loren T., and David Noel Freedman, "The Fragments of a Targum to Leviticus in Qumran Cave 4 (4Q156): A Linguistic Comparison and Assessment." Pages 79-95 *Targum and Scripture: Studies in Aramaic Translations and Interpretation in Memory of Ernest G. Clarke.* Studies in the Aramaic Interpretation of Scripture 2. Edited by Paul V. M. Flesher. Leiden: Brill, 2002.

Talmon, Shemarayahu. "Was the Book of Esther Known At Qumran?" *Dead Sea Discoveries* 2.3 (1995): 249-67.

Tappy, Ron E. "Tel Zayit and the Tel Zayit Abededary in Their Regional Context." Pages 1-44 in Ron E. Tappy and P. Kyle McCarter. *Literate Culture and Tenth-Century Canaan: The Tel Zayit Abecedary in Context.* Winona Lake, IN: Eisenbrauns, 2008.

Tawil, Hayim and Bernard Schneider. *Crown of Aleppo: The Mystery of the Oldest Hebrew Bible Codex.* Philadelphia: JPS, 2010.

Tigay, Jeffery. *Empirical Models for Biblical Criticism.* Philadelphia: University of Pennsylvania Press, 1985.

———. *You Shall Have No Other Gods: Israelite Religion in the Light of Hebrew Inscriptions.* Harvard Semitic Studies 31. Atlanta: Scholars Press, 1986.

Tov, Emanuel. *The Text-Critical Use of the Septuagint in Biblical Reseach*. 3d ed. Eisenbrauns, 2015.

Toorn, Karel van der. *Scribal Culture and the Making of the Hebrew Bible*. Cambridge, MA: Harvard University Press, 2007.

Tov, Emanuel. *Textual Criticism of the Hebrew Bible*. 3d rev. and exp. ed. Minneapolis: Fortress, 2012.

Turner, Fredrick Jackson. "The Significance of History." *Wisconsin Journal of Education* 21.10 (1891): 230-34.

Vasholz, Robert I. "4QTargumJob versus 11QTargum Job." *Revue de Qumran* 11.1 (1982): 109.

Van De Mieroop, Marc. *A History of the Ancient Near East ca. 3000-323 BC*. 2d ed. Malden, MA: Blackwell, 2007.

_____. *A History of Ancient Egypt*. Malden, MA: Blackwell, 2011.

Van Dijk, Jacobus. "The Amarna Period and the Later New Kingdom. Pages 272-313 in *The Oxford History of Ancient Egypt*. Edited by Ian Shaw. Oxford: Oxford University Press, 2000.

Veldhuis, Niek. "Levels of Literacy." Pages 68-89 in *The Oxford Handbook of Cuneiform Culture*. Edited by Karen Radner and Eleanor Robson. Oxford: Oxford University Press, 2011.

Waltke, Bruce K. "Old Testament Textual Criticism." Pages 156-86 in *Foundations for Biblical Interpretation*. Edited by D. S. Dockery, Kenneth A. Matthews, and Tobert Sloan. Nashville: Broadman & Holman, 1994.

Walton, John. *The Lost World of Genesis One: Ancient Cosmology and the Origins Debate*. DownersGrove, IL: InterVartisy, 2009.

————. *Ancient Near Eastern Thought and the Old Testament: Introducing the Conceptual World of the Hebrew Bible*. 2nd ed. Grand Rapids, MI: Baker, 2018.

Weiss, Judy. "The Masorah of The Jewish Theological Seminary of America Library Manuscript 232 (E. N. Adler Ms. 346)." Ph.D. Diss. The Jewish Theological Seminary, 2009

Weinberg, Bella Hass. "Citation, Obliteration, and Plagiarism, as Discussed in Ancient Jewish Sources." *Journal of the American Society for Information Science and Technology* 61. Issue 11 (November 2010): 2337-64.

Wellhausen, Julius. *Prolegomena to the History of Ancient Israel.* New York: Meridian Books, 1957.

Wilson, Jonathan R. "Canon and Theology: What is at Stake?" Pages 241-54 in *Exploring the Origins of the Bible: Canon Formation in Historical, Literary, and Theological Perspective.* Craig A. Evans and Emanuel Tov, eds. Grand Rapids, MI: Baker, 2008.

Wollenberg, Rebecca Scharbach. "The Dangers of Reading as We Know It: Sight Reading as a Source of Heresy in Early Rabbinic Traditions." *Journal of the American Academy of Religion* 85.3 (2017)" 709–745.

Yancey, Philip. *The Bible Jesus Read.* Grand Rapids, MI: Zondervan, 1999.

Yardeni, Ada. *The Book of Hebrew Script: History, Paleography, Script Styles, Calligraphy, and Design.* 3rd ed. Jerusalem: Carta, 2010.

Yeivin, Israel. *Introduction to the Tiberian Masorah.* Translated and edited by E. J. Revell. Masoretic Studies 5. Missoula, MT: Scholars Press, 1980.

Young, Ian. *Diversity in Pre-Exilic Hebrew. Forschungen zum Alten Tetamentum* 5. Tübingen: Mohr Siebeck, 1993.

Zakovitch, Yair. *An Introduction to Inner-Biblical Interpretation.* Even Yehudah: Rekhes hotsa'ah le-or, proyeḳṭim ḥinukhiyim, 1992. (Heb.)

———. "Inner-Biblical Interpretation" in Ronald Hendel, ed., *Reading Genesis: Ten Methods.* Cambridge: Cambridge University Press, 2010.

Made in the USA
Middletown, DE
25 August 2023

37189567R00086